Haunted Highways
and
Ghostly Travelers

Christopher E. Wolf

4880 Lower Valley Road, Atglen, Pennsylvania 19310

Cover photo: street corner © Zeljka Burazin. www.bigstockphoto.com.

text by Christopher E. Wolf
photos by author unless otherwise noted in the text

Schiffer Books are available at special discounts for bulk purchases for sales promotions or premiums. Special editions, including personalized covers, corporate imprints, and excerpts can be created in large quantities for special needs. For more information contact the publisher:

Published by Schiffer Publishing Ltd.
4880 Lower Valley Road
Atglen, PA 19310
Phone: (610) 593-1777; Fax: (610) 593-2002
E-mail: Info@schifferbooks.com

For the largest selection of fine reference books on this and related subjects, please visit our website at **www.schifferbooks.com**
We are always looking for people to write books on new and related subjects. If you have an idea for a book please contact us at the above address.

This book may be purchased from the publisher.
Include $5.00 for shipping.
Please try your bookstore first.
You may write for a free catalog.

In Europe, Schiffer books are distributed by
Bushwood Books
6 Marksbury Ave.
Kew Gardens
Surrey TW9 4JF England
Phone: 44 (0) 20 8392 8585; Fax: 44 (0) 20 8392 9876
E-mail: info@bushwoodbooks.co.uk
Website: www.bushwoodbooks.co.uk

Disclaimer and Acknowledgment of Trademarks

All views are expressed by individuals and are not meant to be associated with any official National Park Service facility or historic site. This book is derived from the author's independent research.

Copyright © 2011 by Christopher E. Wolf

Library of Congress Control Number: 2011930182

All rights reserved. No part of this work may be reproduced or used in any form or by any means—graphic, electronic, or mechanical, including photocopying or information storage and retrieval systems—without written permission from the publisher.
The scanning, uploading and distribution of this book or any part thereof via the Internet or via any other means without the permission of the publisher is illegal and punishable by law. Please purchase only authorized editions and do not participate in or encourage the electronic piracy of copyrighted materials.
"Schiffer," "Schiffer Publishing Ltd. & Design," and the "Design of pen and inkwell" are registered trademarks of Schiffer Publishing Ltd.

Designed by RoS
Type set in Bergell LET/Zurich BT

ISBN: 978-0-7643-3895-3

Printed in The United States of America

Dedications

First and foremost I'd like to dedicate this book to my lovely and understanding wife, Cindy, who has faithfully stuck with me through all the ups and downs of our life as this volume was being written.

Acknowledgments

It takes a lot of people to make an idea for a book turn into reality. I know I've said that before, but it doesn't make it any less true now. First, I'd like to thank my editor at Schiffer Publishing, Dinah Roseberry. Secondly, I'd like to thank the library system of Lancaster County. Without their vast resources of information, this book would've been a lot harder to write. Thirdly, I like to thank all of my readers who have supported these modest attempts at entertaining people with my paranormal anecdotes over the last few years. Finally, and most importantly, I'd like to give my love and thanks to my wonderful wife, Cindy. She may not be the author of this book, but she has contributed to its existence more than anyone can imagine.

CONTENTS

Introduction...6

Section One
Haunted Roads and Spectral Streets
- The Schwartz Frau and the Weiss Frau of Adamstown ...12
- Seattle's Underground Street Girl ...18
- The Twin Tunnels of Downingtown ...29
- Gravity Hills ...33
- Las Vegas' Haunted Streets ...36
- The Ghostly Baker of St. Peter's Village ...41
- Does John Brown's Spirit Haunt the Streets of Harper's Ferry? ...45

Section Two
Railroad Wraiths
- Does Big John Still Haunt the Big Bend Tunnel? ...54
- Abraham Lincoln's Funeral Train (New York Central Railroad Tracks) ...57
- The Haunted Tracks of the Yukon and White Pass Railroad ...59
- Specters of the Strasburg Railroad ...63

Section Three
Cursed Cars and Phantom Vehicles
- The Crazed Driver ...70
- The Little Bastard – James Dean's Death Car ...71
- Phantom Stagecoaches ...75
- The Phantom Ford of Netherland Inn Road ...81

Section Four
Ghost Ships
- Ghosts of the Titanic ...84
- The Queen Mary ...92

Section Five
Haunted Bridges
- Sachs Mill Bridge in Gettysburg ...98
- The Temptress of Old Birdsboro Bridge ...103
- Cry-Baby Bridges ...108

Section Six
Ghostly Hitchhikers
- Midnight Mary of Bordentown Road ...112
- The Green Ghost Girl of Ireland ...119

Section Seven
Aircraft Apparitions
- Flight 401 ...128
- Shannon Airport's Fairy Ring ...131

Section Eight
Too Strange to Classify!
- The Bermuda Triangle ...136
- The Greenbriar Light ...141
- The St. Augustine Lighthouse ...146

Appendix A
A Word About Orbs and Other Photographic Anomalies ...152

Appendix B
Ghost Tours ...154

Sources
Bibliography...157

Places Index...158

Introduction

Ghosts and hauntings come in many different forms. Most of us, when we think of a haunting it usually involves a dilapidated old house, a creepy looking mansion or castle in England, or in the case of Gettysburg, a whole little town surrounded by a tragic, massive battlefield.

But, in the years of doing paranormal research, I've repeatedly come across accounts of hauntings, specters, and ghosts of a different sort from your typical house-bound spirits. These ghosts are more inclined to haunt the outdoors. They prefer the open road, the high seas, and riding the rails.

What exactly is a ghost? Is it the life force of a the deceased? Could it be a psychic imprint of an emotionally charged moment in time that mindlessly repeats itself over and over until it runs out of energy? Or is it something else entirely alien to what we know as life?

Ghosts or spirits, call them what you will, are actually all of the above and more! Science has yet to explain what a ghost is, so at this point, really all anybody can do is speculate and guess. One thing that has been done by paranormal investigators is to classify some of the different types of hauntings that people have experienced over the years.

So what are the different types of ghosts and hauntings out there? Whether you believe in ghosts or are a skeptic like many of the ghost hunters in the field today, most paranormal investigators tend to agree on the classifications of some spirits.

There are several types of hauntings that are of a similar nature; these have been grouped into different categories such as: Interactive Hauntings, Residual Hauntings, Poltergeists, and a category specifically for this book: Phantom Vehicles.

Interactive Hauntings

An interactive haunting is a paranormal event where the spirit actually acknowledges the presence of the living and interacts intelligently with them either by talking, asking questions, or answering questions themselves. Sometimes the spirit appears so lifelike that the person doesn't even know that they're talking to a ghost. A good example of this type of haunting is the numerous "Vanishing Hitchhiker" tales, such as Resurrection Mary in Chicago.

Residual Hauntings

A residual haunting, on the other hand, has no two-way communication. The entity of this phenomenon will usually have no awareness of witnesses and usually repeats the same scene over and over whether anyone is paying attention to it or not. President Lincoln's funeral train making it's annual, nocturnal route is a good example of a residual haunting.

Poltergeist

A poltergeist is a very rare type of haunting usually associated with a home or a place of business that focuses on a teen or young adult who subconsciously either attracts or causes to manifest a spirit or entity that causes pranks, noises, and in extreme cases, even physical harm to the property and people in their vicinity. Since this is a book about traveling spirits and haunted highways, it's very hard to pin down a poltergeist for these locations.

Most poltergeist are very territorial, although in the case of the Bell Witch, the poltergeist was known to manifest itself on the road outside the Bell homestead when it caused President Andrew Jackson's wagon wheels to lock-up as proof of it's existence to him.

Phantom Vehicles

...Which brings me to our last category: Phantom Vehicles. Phantom Vehicles, too, are very tricky for a paranormal investigator to pin down for an investigation. Unlike haunted locations, a phantom vehicle can appear anywhere, or as several different types of transportation, usually in the form of cars, trucks, planes, and even ships.

At this point, we're not even sure why they exist. Is a deceased person connected to the vehicle causing it to manifest in spirit form? Or is the vehicle itself taking on a an afterlife of its own? What makes Phantom vehicles so unique in the paranormal world is that they are intimate objects that seem to appear as ghosts themselves, unlike a house being haunted by a spirit. The vehicles are the spirits.

A prime example of what is meant by a phantom vehicle is described in a case in Garden City, Long Island, where a suspected ghost car was chased by the local police and ended up going through a fence without crashing through it ... effectively ending the police car's pursuit.

All over the world there have been accounts of ghostly hitchhikers, ghosts ships and Phantom Vehicles. With as much time and the amount of traveling that people do, is it any wonder that there are so many paranormal occurrences involving highways, railroads, and airplanes? Usually, a tragic and unexpected death can trigger a haunting. I can't think of any way that is more tragic and unexpected than dying from a vehicular accident.

All my life I've had the chance to reflect on how close I've come to being one of these spirits. At the age of four, I was involved in a near-fatal car accident when I ran out into the middle of the street chasing a ball. I tripped over a newly placed manhole cover and before I could stand up and get out of the street, a car ran me over. The car's front bumper caught me right under my chin and dragged me down the street for half a block before the horrified driver realized he had run over a child and not a ball.

A lot of times it's difficult for me and other paranormal investigators and even other writers of the paranormal accounts to truly understand what these confused and sad entities might be going through in their afterlife existence. It's hard to really get into the mind of a Revolutionary war soldier about to die in battle or a American Civil War private facing down a cannonball. But, the tragic spirits in this book are much more emotionally accessible. We all ride some form of transportation or have walked along a street or a road. Any one of us, at any time due to ill luck could become a one of these sad spirits of the highways and byways.

I've tried to tell some tales of the lesser known spirits that haunt the places of the world that take us from here to there. Some of them are famous in their own part of the world, but many of them are unknown outside of the area they manifest in. To be sure, there are also some very famous ghosts in this book as well. I wanted to give you, the reader a broad overview of the many types of spirits that exist or are reported to have made their presence known across the globe.

SECTION

Haunted Roads

ONE

Almost every city, town, and village in the world has at least one road that the locals consider haunted. Whether they're haunted or not, these roads are invested with the supernatural. Who hasn't wandered down a dark, isolated country road at night and wondered what might be out there lurking in the darkness. From the dawn of time right up to today's urban landscapes of big metropolitan cities, the prospect of what might be out there is always an unsettling and disturbing thought that hides just beneath the surface of our conscious minds, forever ready to spring itself upon us when we least expect or want it to.

Sometimes we've already been alerted to what we should fear on a particular stretch of highway. Perhaps, such as in the case of "Highway 666," its reputation precedes it and we're already expecting some sort of supernatural encounter. Other times we're completely unaware that there's anything out of the ordinary until later when in safety of a roadside diner or motel (and these sometimes play a part in the haunting as well) that we've just had a close encounter with a local haunt.

and Spectral Streets

Sitting on the border of Lancaster and Berks County, Pennsylvania, is the quaint and sleepy little Borough of Adamstown. Known as the self-styled antiques capital of the world, there truly is a large number of antique shops in the small area.

Main Street in Adamstown where ghostly women, dogs, and headless pigs roam around town.

Not only is Adamstown a large antique venue, but if you're looking for a hat, look no further because one of the largest hat factories, Bollman Hats, is right on the edge of town.

For such a small town, Adamstown does have its share of history. Founded on July 4th, 1761, by William Addams, it was built on the site of a Native American Village and was originally called "Addamsburry." They've even got some veterans of the Civil War buried in the town graveyard.

Several unusual spirits make their presence known on Main Street. There's two female spirits, a friendly black ghost dog, and a whole herd of ghostly pigs!

ONE

Two of the most well-known spirits are the Weiss Frau and the Schwartz Frau—which in Pennsylvania Dutch language means The White Lady and the Black Lady. This isn't about their skin pigment but refers to the color of their dresses. They can be very difficult to pin down to a location on Main Street as they are known to appear anywhere along the street and at anytime of the day or night.

One thing that is known for certain about them is they have some very peculiar habits. For one thing, they are never very far apart from one another when they appear on the street. I've had a few local residents of the town tell me that many times they can be seen near the little park and gazebo on Main Street just east of the school.

Regardless of where the two ghostly ladies are spotted, they have the distinction of being so rude as to not gaze upon one another, or anyone who might pass by them for that matter. It seems as though they're in their own little world.

It would be easy to classify them as a residual haunting except for the fact that they do seem aware of their surroundings and just choose not to interact with other pedestrians or each other.

People have been known to try and follow them down Main Street to see where they are so intent on going. Ah! And where do they go you might ask? Why, where any self-respecting ghost in town would go...to the Cedar Grove Cemetery just north of Main Street. Once inside the small town cemetery they will both pause as if contemplating some secret known only to them and then vanish into thin air without so much as a goodbye wave.

The ghostly Frau's are always walking to this cemetery. No one knows why.

SECTION

I had the opportunity to work for four years in Adamstown at Bujno Pottery, which is on the west end of Adamstown. I didn't live in Adamstown, but I spent a significant amount of waking hours there over those four years and I had the chance to look around the town on many occasions. I would frequently take my lunch break and walk to the center of town past the Post Office and the VFW building.

During my mid-day walk, I had chance to talk with many of the people who lived there. Some of them were relatively newcomers, but others had lived there all their lives and wouldn't have it any other way. Most of the native Adamstowners had heard of the twin spirits and some of them had family members or friends who actually claimed to have seen the dark and light spirits over the years.

I, unfortunately, had no such luck during the years I worked in town. Once I had heard about these wandering spirits, I'll admit I always tried to keep an eye out for them as I walked along Main Street, but perhaps they just didn't feel comfortable appearing to an outsider such as myself.

Pass through this arch and you might have a paranormal encounter with two ghostly ladies.

ONE

Ghost Pigs Anyone?

I've come across many different types of headless helicopter pilots and a variety of headless horsemen in the course of my paranormal investigations and in doing research for my previous two books, but I've never, ever come across headless ghost pigs.

Back in the late 1800s, on the site where Bollman's Hat Factory now sits on the eastern edge of Main Street, there was a butcher shop and a distillery. The Entenach Distillery used grain to make alcohol and then they would throw the spent grain over to the Butcher shops where they kept a supply of hogs who would naturally feed on the grain and grow plumper and fatter. This plan worked out wonderfully for the butcher and it also allowed the distillery to easily get rid of tons and tons of useless spent grain at no cost. A symbiotic relationship that befitted everyone... except the hogs.

It was claimed that the grain-fattened hogs were so much in demand, that the Butcher's business prospered and he had slaughtered so many

It's on this spot where thousands of pigs were slaughtered, causing some of their specters to roam headlessly down Main Street.

pigs that the street literally was filled at times with herds of headless phantom swines! Looking at all the quaint Victorian houses lining Main Street, it was hard for me to imagine the reaction local residents would've had looking at such a spectacle from the safety of their front porches.

Fortunately, for the hogs, the Entenach Distillery and the Butcher shop were bought by a hat company near the turn of the century. The

hat company used the distillery as part of the factory until it could build a larger facility that now sits right on Main Street. The butcher shop is long gone; most likely it's part of the parking lot for the Bollman Hat employees.

Since Bollman's took over the land, there have been no more reports of headless ghost hogs roaming the streets. Perhaps with the end of the butchering, the spirits of the pigs could finally be put to rest.

The Black Dog Ghost

On lighter note, there is one other spirit that manifests itself on Main Street in Adamstown, and unlike the ghost pigs and The Frau's, this spirit is sighted more frequently. Again, this spirit is an animal. It takes the form of a black dog. Conflicting reports say that it's a black Labrador puppy and others aren't as sure of what breed it is.

Black ghost dogs have been sighted all over the world. The most famous of these canine specters is recounted in the Sherlock Holmes story: "The Hound of The Baskervilles." The hound in that story was typical of most black ghost dog sightings. It was considered an evil omen and would announce the death of a member of the Baskerville Family by its appearance.

The Black dog of Adamstown has a completely different aura to it. It appears friendly by all accounts. Most people who have spotted it don't even realize it might not be a real dog, because it looks solid and not ghostly.

I may have had encounter with the black dog several years ago when I was working in Adamstown. I was taking my usual lunchtime walk down Main Street past the School on my way to the Post Office, when I took notice to a black dog across the street from me. It was heading west along the street and I was going east. It did nothing out of the ordinary and didn't pay any attention to me as it wandered through front yards as dogs will do. I didn't see anyone with a leash nearby, but in a small town with little traffic, some people let their dogs wander ahead of them. I didn't really take notice if it had a collar or not. I continued on my way to the Post Office, mailed my letters, and headed back to work. I did mention to the clerk that I saw a black dog running loose and suggested they might want to keep an eye out for it, in case it was someone's pet that had gotten loose.

ONE

I tried to see if I could find the dog on my way back to work, but I saw no sign of it. I asked a few people as I passed them if they'd seen the dog and they hadn't. I had to get back to work and couldn't take any more time looking for the mysterious black dog. Had I known about the legend of the Black Dog of Adamstown, I would've taken a longer lunch break and gone hunting for it.

I only found out later that I might have encountered the ghost dog when a neighbor of the Pottery Studio who knew I was into the paranormal gave me a copy of an Article in the *Reading Eagle Newspaper* by Charles J. Adams about the ghosts of Adamstown, and it mentioned the black ghost dog.

So, if you ever happen to visit Adamstown, and I highly recommend a visit if you're in the Pennsylvania Dutch area, that high-pitched squeal you hear on Main Street might not be a driver taking a high-speed turn...

> To get to Adamstown: From Lancaster, PA—Take U.S. 222 North towards Ephrata/Reading. Take the Denver exit, then turn left onto Spur Road. Take a slight right turn onto PA 272 (N. Reading Road). Adamstown will be a few miles up the road on your left.

SECTION 2

Seattle's Underground Street Girl

One of the most popular cities to visit in the Pacific Northwest is Seattle. This eclectic city is located in the state of Washington. In the late 1800s, it was a jumping off point for many miners and fortune seekers heading to Alaska to strike it rich in the Klondike Gold Rush. Seattle has a varied and sometimes violent history, not to mention quite a few ghosts and hauntings.

Chief Seattle, whom the city was named after, stated in a famous speech to the settlers who had taken the native American's land that, "The dead are not altogether powerless." He further cautioned them to beware, "For at night, when the streets of your cities and villages shall be silent, and you think them deserted, they will throng with the returning hosts that once filled and still love this beautiful land."

Seattle had been inhabited by Native Americans for almost 4,000 years, but all that

A close up of the monument to Chief Seattle for whom the city of Seattle is named after. *Courtesy of Cindy Wolf*

ONE

was about to change in 1851. White settlers, fulfilling what they called "Manifest Destiny" (which was a name the U.S. Government gave to what was essentially, white settlers taking land away from the indigenous Native Americans already living there).

One of the first groups of settlers was the Denny Party, (not to be confused with the Denny's Restaurant chain), led by Arthur A. Denny. They settled into the area that is now part of downtown Seattle, while at the same time, further south, David Swinson "Doc" Maynard and his group settled in.

The Native American tribes that had occupied the land for many thousands of years didn't just give up their land peacefully. It took five years, but finally they were pushed to the breaking point and decided to strike back. Unfortunately, it was an ill-fated attempt. What is now known as the Battle of

The Chief Seattle monument as it sits in Pioneer Square. *Courtesy of Cindy Wolf*

SECTION

Seattle took place in 1856. The settlers with the help of the sloop, *Decatur* and a contingent of U.S. Marines from the ship, repelled the attack with only the loss of two settlers' lives. The Native Americans didn't fare as well. They claimed that twenty-eight of their warriors died and another eighty were wounded.

A far more devastating halt to the growth of Seattle occurred thirty-three years after the Battle of Seattle and the settlers had no one to blame but themselves for their misfortune.

The roots of this disaster started thirty-nine years earlier. Because of the easy access to lumber, most, if not all, of the businesses and homes were solely made of wood. To further add fuel to this disaster, not only were the buildings made of wood, but so was the sewer and water system.

On June 6th, 1889, the greatest disaster in Seattle's history commenced: The Great Seattle Fire. What started as a simple accident, quickly became a full-blown tragedy.

This is a section of the wooden water system which helped fuel The Great Seattle Fire. *Courtesy of Cindy Wolf*

ONE

A 24-year-old Swedish immigrant named John E. Beck (or Back, as some reports state) was cooking some balls of glue over a gasoline fire in Clairmont's Cabinet-Making shop located at the intersection of Front Street and Madison Avenue. The glue accidentally started boiling over and caught fire. The hardy Swede reacted quickly and tried in vain to stop the blaze from spreading by dousing it with a bucket of water. Unfortunately for the city of Seattle, this was the wrong thing to do, although he had only the best intentions.

What happened next can only be described as an unfortunate series of events. When young John doused the burning glue with water, it caused a chain reaction. The burning glue quickly spread to a pile of wood chips and cans of turpentine that were nearby on the floor, which quickly added fuel to the already rapidly growing fire.

To the credit of the Seattle Volunteer Fire Company, they tried their best to contain the fire, but the odds were stacked against them from the beginning. There had already been a drought that summer and there was

the fact that most of the buildings were constructed of wood (there were no firewalls back then). Added to the mix were fire hydrants with very poor water pressure placed on every other street. Now you had the formula for the perfect storm...a *firestorm* to be exact.

So, what started as a small industrial shop fire, quickly bloomed into a raging inferno. By the next morning, June 7th, more than twenty-five city blocks had been decimated by the fire.

You might think that with a fire of this magnitude there would be a large fatality list and you'd be right. Only it wasn't what you might think. Only one person lost their life in the blaze, a youth by the name of James Goin. On the other hand, it was reported that millions of rats and other vermin had died in the fire. Whew! Talk about urban renewal!

The saying goes that *fire is cleansing* and that seemed to be the case for Seattle. Almost immediately from the ashes of the fire a new Seattle would rise like a phoenix. The citizen's committee held a meeting and several improvements were implemented in the next few weeks that would change the landscape of the city of Seattle forever.

One of the biggest changes was that all of the buildings had to be made of brick or stone. (No surprise there.) Another change was that they decided to raise the level of the city streets by one story. What this meant was that now the second floor of a building would actually be the street level and the first floor would be underground.

For some time it made walking across the street difficult at best. Because of doing the re-leveling at the same time, they chose to do the streets before the sidewalks were raised. People actually had to walk up ladders to reach the street and then had to climb back down them on the other side. Eventually, the sidewalks were brought up to the street level, and as a result of this re-grading, a vast underground "city" of streets was created and still exists beneath Seattle to this day.

Orbs Aplenty

But enough of the history. Here's the paranormal scoop on this labyrinth of underground streets. When my wife, Cindy, and I went on an Alaskan cruise a few years ago, we chose Seattle as our port of departure and decided to arrive a couple of days early so we could do some sightseeing and perhaps a paranormal investigation or two.

ONE

Many ghostly encounters have occurred in this dark, dank "City" under Seattle. You can even see three orbs! *Courtesy of Cindy Wolf*

I had heard of the Seattle Underground tour before we left home and felt that it would be a great place to do an investigation. Cindy agreed and was looking forward to getting some unique photos with her new Kodak M381 camera, that she bought specifically for our trip to Alaska. With twelve mega pixels, we were sure to get some very clear pictures and hopefully a few paranormal ones as well.

The Underground Tour actually starts out above ground in the heart of Seattle's Pioneer Square in Doc Maynard's Public House. It's here that you buy your tickets for the Underground Tour. Be forewarned, the tour is for adults only due to the adult subject matter and no one under the age of 18 is even able to go on the tour. They only take cash for tickets (at the writing of this book), so you had better make a trip to the ATM to get some before waiting in line to buy your tickets.

With ticket in hand, you're herded into a large Victorian era room complete with huge mirror-backed bar and chandeliers hanging from the ceiling. While we waited for the crowd of people to gather and take their seats in the room, Cindy took some preliminary pictures of the room and to our surprise, she managed to capture some "orbs" in this area. For those of you who aren't familiar with what orbs are, I'd like to a moment to discuss them and how they relate to the paranormal.

SECTION

You can see a lot of orbs in Doc. Maynard's Public House. This is the room where the Underground Tours begin. *Courtesy of Cindy Wolf*

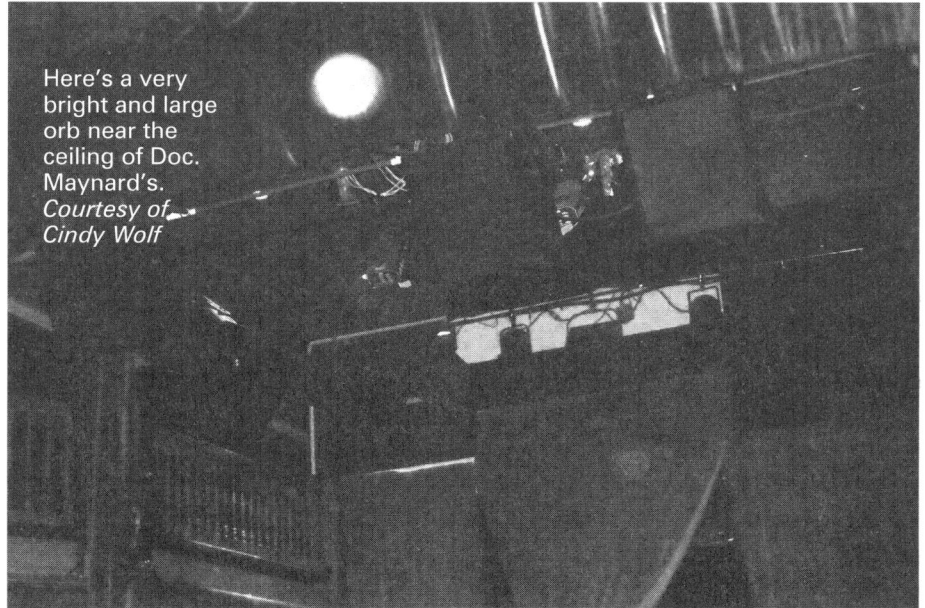

Here's a very bright and large orb near the ceiling of Doc. Maynard's. *Courtesy of Cindy Wolf*

ONE

Orbs are glowing balls of light that appear in various sizes, brightnesses, and colors in photographs or on video. When I first started paranormal investigating over a decade ago with the Pennsylvania Ghost Hunter's Society, orbs were just being newly discovered—mainly because digital Photography was in its infancy back then and not many people had access to a digital camera and most orb pictures were digital in nature... most of them, but not all of them. How do I know this? Because for many years I worked part-time in a photo lab and developed and printed many thousands of pictures on a daily basis. This was before digital pictures were common (we didn't even have a digital film processor until years later). I saw quite a few orb pictures that were developed from regular rolls of film. Granted the majority of them were probably from natural flash anomalies reflecting off mundane objects, but that still didn't account for *all* of them.

I've visited several websites and have heard other paranormal investigators say that they don't consider orbs as valid proof of the paranormal. This is mainly because they claim that it's very easy to fake an orb picture with dust, smoke, or some other artificial means. Even if it's not a willful deception on the part of the photographer, they blame low resolution digital cameras or naturally occurring particles of dust, insects, or water vapor that look like orbs because of camera flash or other mechanical or software failures.

It's great to be skeptical, in fact, in paranormal investigating its a requirement...to a degree. A healthy dose of skepticism never hurts an investigation, but too much can actually be detrimental. I prefer to remain as objective as possible during an investigation. I treat investigations differently than I do when I'm writing a book on hauntings where I'm more interested in telling an entertaining story, than relating cold hard facts. So do I believe every orb picture I see is proof of the paranormal? Of course not, even some of my own orb pictures I've dismissed as invalid or questionable and haven't used in any of my books. So just because some orb pictures are non-paranormal in nature doesn't mean they all are.

Now that I've had my chance to talk about orbs, let's get back to the story... So we took some pictures while inside Doc Maynard's Public House while waiting to go on our tour of Seattle's underground streets. Cindy did get a few orbs in her photos and we've included them here for you to judge.

Next, we were split into several smaller groups of about fifteen people and assigned a tour guide. Our guide was a young, brown-haired woman who, as a true Seattlite was clutching a cup of Starbucks coffee as she led our group down into the dank and gloomy recesses of the Seattle Underground.

As our eyes adjusted to the dim light, you could see what at first looked like someone's unfinished basement. There was an old bar, a round plush couch that looked like it might once have wrapped around a pillar in some Victorian-era salon, and lots of cement rubble scattered about the room. But what made this unique is that even though it looked like someone's junk-strewn man cave, it really was a time capsule of another era in time. It was very ghost townish.

After exiting this room through a doorway, we walked into a twisty, curving corridor that looked like an old city street, except for the fact that instead of sky above us, there was a cob-webbed, wooden beam-supported ceiling that was mainly made of mortared brick, but on occasion was made of a strange-looking purple-colored glass. We later found out the glass was meant to be a skylight to allow sunlight down into the depths back in the 1800s, but over the centuries, the glass had turned purple with age and didn't seem to give off much light.

Cindy and many other people in our group started taking pictures of the weird, dark world we had entered. I was more interested in hearing the details from our guide about how strange the underground city had become over the years. While walking through the tunnels and dark streets we would see signs for various businesses still painted on the walls although the only people seeing them would no longer be customers.

Our guide led us through the maze of tunnels and would occasionally stop and stand on a piece of rubble and explain how life back in the early days of Seattle differed from today. One of the funniest stories was about how bad the potholes on the early roads were. There was a newspaper article from the late 1800s showing someone with a rowboat actually fishing in one of the expansive potholes, and there was a second more serious article about a 10-year-old boy who actually fell in one of the more treacherous holes and drowned.

One thing was for certain, that no matter what their social status, people from all walks of life who lived in Seattle had one thing in common: They all had to deal with the bad roads and streets.

ONE

A Sewing Circle Ghost

After we finished our several-hour tour, Cindy and I decided to get some lunch at a nearby Irish Pub, named FADO. It was while we were waiting for our food order and I was enjoying a local micro brew that Cindy came across one of the best paranormal pictures we had ever taken.

One of the stories that our guide had talked about on the tour was how there was quite a busy brothel service that flourished in the Seattle underground during the 1800s, and that in order to sound better in the public eye, they did what many spin doctors do for people's reputations today. They lied. Instead of calling them prostitutes, they called them "seamstresses" and a brothel was known as a "sewing circle."

Cindy looked startled for a second and then held her camera out to me. "Take a look at this and tell me what you see."

I took the small camera and stared at the three- by four-inch LED screen. At first I wasn't sure what I was looking for and then I saw "her." Cindy smiled as I handed her back the camera.

"Did you see her?" she asked. I was stunned. This had to have been the best ghost photo we'd ever taken up to now.

This is our best ghost photo yet! You can see a female apparition in the lower right corner of the wall. *Courtesy of Cindy Wolf*

SECTION

What I saw and what Cindy confirmed was a faint image of a young girl or woman wearing a large floppy hat reminiscent of ones worn by women in the late 1800s to early 1900s. What was even more bizarre and amazing was that only the top half of the girl was visible in the picture. Her bottom half was non-existent because her head and torso were above the level of the floor. She had a very hazy, blurry look to her and you could tell right away that you weren't looking at a living person. No one on the tour witnessed her image, and just to be sure that it wasn't some trick of the light or some faded poster image on the wall, we actually went back to the spot and checked. We also asked the tour guides in the main building if anyone had a similar picture from that same area. No one did.

We speculated that this picture of Cindy's could be the ghostly manifestation of one of early Seattle's "Seamstresses" still plying her trade after centuries in the underground domain of Seattle. So if you ever get to Seattle and have a chance to go on the Underground Tour. Keep an eye out. You might have more members in your tour group than what you started with.

Seattle is in the state of Washington in the Pacific Northwest. To get to the Underground Tour, take your best route to Pioneer Square. The Underground Tour starts at Doc Maynard's Public House located at 608 First Avenue, between Cherry Street and Yesler Way.

The Twin Tunnels of Downingtown

Tunnels have always had a creepy vibe to them. There's just something unsettling about crawling around in a dark, musty, wet tunnel that sends shivers down your spine. Maybe it's the way sounds get distorted and echo off the walls.

This is the scene of a grisly unsolved murder. *Courtesy of Cindy Wolf*

The Twin Tunnels located in Downingtown, Pennsylvania, not only exude darkness (even in the daytime), but have several tragic tales of death and murder associated with them. Enough to have the area once called "The Murderous Mile" many years ago. It has also generated several ghost stories associated with this stretch of highway.

Located on Valley Creek Road, near Boot Road, the Twin Tunnels of Downingtown have spawned numerous tales of hauntings. Although they're called the "Twin Tunnels," there's actually three of them.

Most of the hauntings associated with these odd tunnels have to do with violent death: Hangings, murders, and suicides surround these tunnels like a malignant aura.

The tunnels have a long history that stretches back all the way to 1912. They were built for the railroad in order for trains to cross over the tops of the tunnels,

and some trains still do to this day. The tunnels weren't always known as the Twin Tunnels. For many years they had a very different name – a name actually more suited to their dark nature. Due to the unsafe working conditions while constructing the tunnels for the railroad, they were known as the "Murderous Mile."

It seems that while excavating, there were so many cave-ins that many of the Irish railroad laborers were crushed to death. Back then, there were no labor laws and life was hard and cheap. These poor unfortunates never got a proper burial and were interred right where they died. No one knows exactly how many of them might still be buried there. So the tunnels had a very dark reputation from the very start of their existence, due to the unrest of the spirits of the Irish railroad laborers. You might think that this alone would make the area a paranormal hot spot, but there's much more tragedy to these foreboding tunnels. The poor workers' spirits are just the tip of the tale of woe surrounding The Twin Tunnels.

The tunnels are not located out in the middle of nowhere. They are on a very busy road, and driving through them can be extremely hazardous if you're not paying attention – it's very easy to get hit by an oncoming vehicle. The reason is simple: The tunnels curve sharply and you can't see the other side or the approaching traffic. My in-Laws live very close to the Twin Tunnels and I've had to pass through them on many trips to their home. The first time I went through them, Cindy warned me to be careful and had me blow my car horn as a warning to oncoming traffic and flash my headlights before driving through. This strange construction of the tunnels actually plays a part in the ghostly legends surrounding the them.

Short Lives

It's in these dark tunnels a baby's spirit has been heard crying.
Courtesy of Cindy Wolf

In one account, a young woman in the early 1900s (some people say, 1800s, but the tunnels weren't built until 1912) had become pregnant, and not being married caused quite a scandal. Harassed and persecuted, she was unceremoniously run out of town (which town I'm not sure) after giving birth to her illegitimate child. Feeling abandoned, guilty, and painfully desperate, the young girl climbed to the top of the hill surrounding the Twin Tunnels. Here's the doubly tragic part: Having run out of options, she took the only path available according to her tortured young mind, and while still holding her new-born infant, she hung herself from the top of the gap between the two tunnels, not only ending her own life, but also her child's.

As the rope tightened around her neck and slowly constricted the life from her, she lost her grip on the infant in her arms and with a sickening thud it fell several stories to it's death on the cold, hard tunnel floor below.

Ever since that tragic day, if you walk into the tunnels at night, (I don't recommend doing this, because of the car traffic), it's said that you can hear the baby crying, and if you're exceptionally lucky, you might even catch a glimpse of the spectral infant lying on the tunnel floor.

Suicide Sounds

In an unrelated, but no less tragic incident, a man was supposed to have also committed suicide by hanging himself from a wire connecting the two tunnels. This other suicide was believed to have happened after the girl had killed herself and her child, but no one has a definite time period for the second suicide. What has been passed on, however, is that if you visit the tunnels and remain very quiet, you can hear the sounds of someone strangling coming from above you. The man's spirit is also supposed to lurk in the shadows of the tunnels.

Suitcase Jane Doe

The most recent tragedy connected to the Twin Tunnels occurred during the summer of 1995 and caused headlines across the country. It was even the subject of the television show: *America's Most Wanted.*

Back in the summer of '95, during an unusual heat wave, while most people were inside trying to keep cool, a fisherman walking along the Brandywine Creek near the Twin Tunnels made a horrific discovery. What he found would set off one of the largest murder investigations in the history of Chester County and make national headline news.

Floating in the shallow water was something wrapped in plastic. Upon close inspection it turned out to be a suitcase. What got his attention wasn't the sight of the strange piece of luggage, but the waves of putrid, decay smell that came from it even wrapped as it was. Sensing something was very wrong, he wasted no time in running to the nearest house and persuading the owners to let him use their phone to call the police.

The fisherman's suspicions were vindicated as soon as the police opened the suitcase. Inside they found the grisly partial remains of a young woman. I say partial because unfortunately it was only her upper body that they initially found. After assuring the public that a full and thorough investigation was underway, they continued to search for the woman's murderer and to find out the identity of the woman.

The media dubbed it "The Pennsylvania Suitcase Jane Doe Case." Over the course of the next ten years, law enforcement officials were able to scrabble together very few clues. They eventually found her legs roughly six months after her torso was discovered. Aside from finding her legs in another county, very little light has been shed on this case. The victim has never been identified and no one has placed a missing persons claim in all these years.

Unfortunately, this case remains unsolved to this day. It's been speculated that the victim was homeless or was from another country. It's also been bandied about that it was a local biker gang that killed the poor woman, but this has never been proven.

On the paranormal side of this murder case, famed TV Psychic Sylvia Browne claimed on *Montel* (the Montel Williams show) that she had received visions of the Jane Doe murder victim, but could give no clues to help law enforcement.

In a 2004 issue of *Eerie Pennsylvania Magazine*, a woman named Katie related her story about her encounter with an apparition at her workplace that greatly resembled the Jane Doe murder victim. According to Katie, she saw the apparition of the woman from only the waist-up several early mornings in a row and at the time was not aware of the Jane Doe Murder Case. Not surprising, Katie's place of employment was the Coatesville Service Building which is located very close to the Brandywine Creek and the Twin Tunnels where the suitcase containing the woman's remains were discovered.

So, the next time you're passing through the Twin Tunnels in Chester County, keep one eye open and your ears peeled… You might just catch a ghostly glimpse from another time.

> The Twin Tunnels are on Valley Creek Road in Downingtown, Pennsylvania. To get there, take Boot Road to Quarry Road, turn right onto Quarry Road which will eventually become Valley Creek Road.

ONE

Gravity hills exist all over the world and a great many of them have a ghostly or urban legend attached to them. A gravity hill is usually a stretch of highway that has a hill on it that ends on a crossroads or a T intersection. What is unusual about them is that even though the road or street is angled at a downhill slope, a car, or anything with wheels will roll back up the hill, seemingly to defy gravity. Sometimes these gravity hills are called Vortexes and are supposed to be gateways to otherworldly dimensions.

School Kids on a Mission

Hershey, Pennsylvania

My first encounter with a gravity hill took place as I was researching locations for my first book: *Ghosts of Hershey and Vicinity*. That gravity hill had a ghostly legend attached to it that told of a bus load of school children having run off an embankment on the other side of the road opposite this hill. Some of the children died in the accident and it is said that the spirits of these students are responsible for the phenomenon by pushing vehicles back up the hill to keep anyone else from suffering their tragic fate.

Battalion, Alabama

Some gravity hills are near railroad tracks or bridges. For example, in Battalion, Alabama, there's a wooden bridge where locals say a school bus load of children had an accident and crashed off the bridge into the lake. For many years, people have claimed that if you drive your car to the bridge at night and stop with the front tires resting on the right side of the bridge and then put your car into neutral, the ghosts of the children of the school bus accident will push your car across so you don't suffer the same fate as they did. Not so different from the legend that I investigated in Pennsylvania.

Mount Hope, Alabama — Henry Hill

In Mount Hope, Alabama, there's a hill called "Henry Hill," and yes, it's another strange vortex/gravity hill, only this one has a different twist to it.

Our tale of tragedy starts in the fall of 1954. According to local historians of the area, a traveling salesman by the name of Henry (no known last name), was making his rounds in his Ford automobile when he developed some kind of engine trouble as he was approaching the town of Mount Hope, Alabama. Evidently, Henry was not too familiar with the country road leading into town or he just plain had no other choice as to where his car decided to conk out; but regardless of why or how, he ended up stopping his car in a low area of the road nicknamed "The Dip."

The Dip has had a bad reputation ever since the early nineteenth century. The Battle of Mount Hope was fought here in 1863, during the Civil War. During the 1940s when government road crews were fixing the roads, they had a problem with County Road 25, which is where The Dip is located. Every time they tried to fill it in, a short time later, it would sink down to it's original level. They eventually gave up. Which turned out to be a bad break for ol' salesman Henry a few years later.

Since his car broke down, Henry had decided to stop at The Dip and to push his car off to the side of the road. Probably not the best spot in the stretch of highway to do this, because unwittingly, he'd stopped his car at a blind spot to other drivers on the road. Any cars following his route would be unable to spot him in The Dip until it was too late.

Just as Henry was pushing his car out of the way, another driver who had been following behind Henry by a few minutes, came cruising down the road at a high rate of speed and was speculated to have been intoxicated behind the wheel. He crested the top of The Dip, and not expecting there to be any obstruction, he was surprised by Henry and his disabled car being right in front of him blocking his path. Frantically, he swerved out of the way and avoided hitting Henry's car. Unfortunately, he struck Henry directly and sadly killed the salesman instantly.

Ironically, if Henry had managed to get his disabled car off the road, he would've probably survived the accident. Now Henry's

ONE

tragic, but vigilant, spirit pushes anyone's car who parks in The Dip and puts their car in neutral back up the hill to avoid his fate.

An alternate version of why Henry's ghost pushes your car up the hill is a totally different story. Another local claims that Henry wasn't a traveling salesman, that he was a local kid who was riding his bike and was hit by a speeding car and pinned up against a tree and died on the spot. Regardless of which story is true, the fact remains that there is a spirit named Henry that haunts The Dip.

> Should you want to experience this Gravity Hill for yourself (and I'm told it always works): Go east on old Highway 24 from Russelville, Alabama. Go towards Moulton, heading east, turn at County Road 23 by a Phillips 66 station. Head south through Mount Hope, and after 1 mile turn right onto County Road 448. Go exactly 2.4 miles. County Road 448 merges into County Road 25, at a sharp turn you have arrived at "The Dip." Put your car in neutral and wait for the ghost of Henry to push you back up the hill.

SECTION 2
Las Vegas' Haunted Streets

You would think with all the bright lights, casinos, nightclubs, and super-mega resort hotels that a place like Las Vegas would be too busy to be haunted, right? You couldn't be more wrong. Even though the city is brightly lit from one end of the strip and doesn't ever seem to darken, there *is* a dark side to Vegas that will never, ever fade away no matter how many times they rebuild.

Tupac Shakur

In 1996, ten years before I ever set foot in Las Vegas, a shooting had occurred. Not that in these violent times this was anything out of the unusual but, on September 7th, a deliberate attack on Tupac Shakur ended his life and gave way to a new urban legend.

Tupac and hundreds, if not thousands, of fight fans were in Las Vegas to witness the fight between Bruce Seldon and Mike Tyson. It was for the World Boxing Heavyweight Title, and in a record 103 seconds, Mike Tyson would regain his title thanks to his bone crunching fist delivering a TKO (Technical Knock Out). To say that Tupac and the other boxing fans were disappointed would be an understatement. At the MGM Grand Hotel and Casino where the fight took place, another fight was just starting as the mob of fans left the area.

Tupac, caught up in the momentum, joined in the mob's fight right outside the entrance to the MGM. Surveillance footage shows him participating in some of the fighting, but he doesn't stick around long at all. Rumor had it that he had a party to go to later that night.

Suge Knight, a good friend of Tupac, loaded him into a brand new black BMW, took him to his hotel room so he could change into more appropriate party clothes and then started to drive him and his posse to a late night private party at Club 662.

Las Vegas has very high traffic all hours of the night, and while it may not seem like a far distance to travel from one end of the city

ONE

to the other, because of this high volume of traffic it can take some time. As they reached the corner of Flamingo and Koval, a white caddy pulled up next to their shiny black BMW. They probably didn't even take a second glance at it, being preoccupied with the coming party.

Without any warning, the windows rolled down on the Cadillac and a hail of gunfire slammed into the black BMW, shattering windows and pumping the interior of the car with a deadly spray of bullets.

Five bullets slammed into Tupac as he tried to reach safety by climbing into the back of the vehicle. Perhaps he might have even had a chance if he was wearing his usual flak vest. But, if you've ever been to Vegas, you know how extremely hot it can get there, even at night. Tupac felt it was too hot to wear the bullet-proof vest, so when the deadly attack took place, he was unprotected.

He fought for life in the hospital for days, and not slightly coincidental, he gave up his life on Friday the 13th.

Just as other celebrities who have died before their time, such as Elvis, James Dean, and Marilyn Monroe, Tupac's fans refuse to believe that he is truly gone. Who knows? Maybe he really is still alive and living under an assumed identity. We'll probably never know. But even if Tupac hasn't been spotted in the flesh, he has been seen in spirit.

Why he would choose to haunt the corner where he was viciously gunned down remains a mystery. It's a popular stop on the Haunted Las Vegas bus tour. There are still some ribbons and offerings hanging off the streetlight near where the attack occurred. At least one resident claims to have seen the ghost of Tupac haunting this spot. Not only does Tupac haunt the spot of his brutal attack, but he is also known to haunt a neighborhood in Vegas near where Mike Tyson used to live.

Benjamin "Bugsy" Siegel Getaway

Another spirit that haunts Las Vegas is not quite the "Gangsta" that Tupac was, but he was in fact a "gangster" literally. It's been said that Benjamin "Bugsy" Siegel still walks around the area near the swimming pools at the Flamingo. Why would he do this and what does it have to do with ghostly travelers? Well, even though Mr.

SECTION 2

Siegel was shot in California as a mob hit, he still had ties to Las Vegas. He was very instrumental in making Vegas as popular as it is today. He loved the *sin city* and he really can't bear to leave even in death. What is interesting to note is that being a gangster, Siegel always knew that he had to be on guard at all times.

A hidden escape car sits somewhere under this monument to Bugsy Segal. Notice the crescent shaped ectoplasm. *Courtesy of Cindy Wolf*

At the original Flamingo Casino Hotel that stood on the site of the current Flamingo, Bugsy had a penthouse apartment that was surrounded by bulletproof glass and even had a secret escape ladder that lead down to a secret garage where a car was supposedly always running with a driver ready to drive at a moments notice in case Siegel had to make a quick getaway. According to a tour guide on the Haunted Las Vegas Ghost Tours, they never did find the secret garage even when they tore up the property when they took down the old Flamingo as they were building the new one. They did, however, salvage some of the unusual gold-plated bath fixtures from Bugsy Siegel's old penthouse apartment and have put them elsewhere on the property.

Since they demolished the old Flamingo in 1996, Bugsy has been seen haunting the rose gardens near the pool where there is a monument to him cast in bronze. It's also near the chapel, and many people have claimed to have seen a man dressed in a tuxedo who bears a striking resemblance to the gangster. Perhaps he's still looking for his hidden underground car to get away.

The Highway of Death

It's no secret that the mob had a large investment in the building of Las Vegas. Six decades ago, the mob used to use a particular road, known as Blue Diamond Road as dumping point to bury bodies that they didn't want found. I think an episode or two of *CSI* mentioned this fact and even had them investigating and solving some decades-old murders.

Blue Diamond Road or Route 160, as it is also known, has another less savory title: The Highway of Death. Not only is it called the Highway of Death because of all the bodies supposedly buried out there, but even in recent times, local residents claim that the stretch of road between Las Vegas and Pahrump is cursed. Back in 2006, no less that seventeen traffic fatalities are attributed to the road.

The Glowing Woman

Perhaps it's all the spirits of murder victims who are buried there that are causing the bad karma. Several ghosts haunt this fifty-mile stretch of highway. On most occasions, the spirits have manifested late at night. None of them seem to be at rest. One particularly active spirit takes the form of glowing woman who likes to surprise drivers by appearing directly in the path of their vehicle and usually forces them to swerve out of the way. Perhaps she is the cause of some of the accidents that have occurred along this stretch of road, and if she isn't, it might just be the poor soul who tries forever to catch a ride...

A Ghostly Hitchhiker

During the early hours of the morning, the apparition of a man tries to get you to stop and give him a ride. A word to the wise, don't stop to pick him up. Then again, maybe some team of ghost hunters should cruise this particular road; they might even capture the evidence they seek.

SECTION 2

A Searching Couple

On nights of a full moon, the ghosts of an older couple have been spotted on the side of the road. It seems as though they are searching for something, but they never find what they're looking for. Perhaps it's the remains of one of the many mob victims, or possibly they themselves might be one of the many nameless souls who are buried out there and they're looking for peace.

On a recent trip to Las Vegas, Cindy and I decided to spend New Years in *sin city* to see how they ring in the new year. We would never think of traveling to Times Square in New York for New Years as neither of us is very fond of the cold, but we felt that Las Vegas would be different – and it was.

We found ourselves people watching at the stroke of midnight, and as we were taking pictures of the many people milling about on the closed strip, Cindy snapped a few pictures that captured quite a few orbs. It seems that even the undead population of Las Vegas still likes to ring in the new year.

Las Vegas is in the State of Nevada.

Should you want to visit the site of Tupac's shooting, it's on the corner of Flamingo Road and Koval Street.

The Current Flamingo Hotel and Casino sits on the site of Bugsy Seagal's original. Just go through the casino till you reach the gardens out back by the pool. There's a small monument to Bugsy and right across from it is the chapel.

Blue Diamond Road is also known as State Route 160. It begins in southern Las Vegas and runs southwest towards Red Rock Canyon and over Mountain Springs Summit, then turns towards Pahrump.

ONE

The Ghostly Baker of St. Peter's Village

The next time you happen to be passing through South Central Pennsylvania, you might want to stop in the picturesque little town of St. Peter's Village. Tucked away from the main road of Route 23, St. Peter's Village is like stepping back to a simpler time, and if you're lucky, you might even meet one of the friendlier spirits associated with those days gone by.

The peaceful village of St. Peters has several spirits walking the streets. *Courtesy of Cindy Wolf*

Used as a way station for the quarry built by Davis Knauer in 1845, St. Peter's Village really came into its own when Knauer built an Inn as a weekend retreat for his family and the quarry workers in the 1880s. Nestled in a small valley and the burbling French Creek below it, St. Peter's Village became a popular tourist destination, and even the Wilmington & Northern Railroad would transport tourists here in the summer to cool off.

SECTION

Three of the village's most active spirits reside at the Inn. *Courtesy of Cindy Wolf*

The intervening years were not so good for the small town however. After the quarry closed, the railroad stopped service to the small resort town, and for a large number of years, it was largely forgotten. It was still a popular watering hole for the locals who were aware of it's existence, though. In later years, it has regained popularity as a relaxing retreat and the St. Peter's Village Inn does a booming business hosting everything from weddings to birthday parties. It's a great place to go just for a Sunday drive. But, there is a dark side to the town and a few ghost stories to boot.

It's on the National Register of Historic places and it definitely looks like a historic town. The buildings are the same as they were in the 1880s when it was first built and there's a town ordinance that states that the outsides of the buildings must remain that way. Walking down the one main street of the town, it's very easy to picture life back in the late nineteenth century. And if you're lucky, you might just run into Herbie the Baker.

Cindy and I visit St. Peter's Village on a regular basis since we don't live too far away. I had been there years ago, but until I started doing research for this particular book I had no idea what ghost stories there were connected to the little village.

Herbie Hinkle

Everyone agrees that Herbie Hinkle, the town Baker, is a great guy. He's the kind of guy who would give a free cookie to small children around town, with a twinkle in his eye. He'd also go out of his way to help someone in need. All in all, Herbie is a gentleman's gentleman and he's also the most friendly ghost in town.

ONE

While he was alive, Herbie lived on the 2nd floor of the St. Peter's Village Inn. According to a history booklet in the St. Peter's Village Bakery, which is next store to the Inn, the current bakery was once the village general store and the village bakery was located on the lower level of this building with the baking ovens facing French Creek. It's here where Herbie Hinkle would've worked. The ovens are no longer there, having been removed ages ago by previous owners, but if you walk down the back

This is where one of Herbie The Baker's oven used to be. *Courtesy of Cindy Wolf*

In Herbie's time, this building was the General Store and town bakery where he baked all his cookies and breads. *Courtesy of Cindy Wolf*

staircase and step out onto the wooden deck underneath the building, you can still see the outline in the red brick wall where the ovens used to be. This is more than likely where Herbie spent most of his time on a daily basis.

SECTION

It's presumed he died of old age, but records are scarce. Most of the time Herbie's spirit is content to hang out at the Inn, but on occasion, he has been known to wander the street and has been spotted on several occasions knocking on doors along St. Peter's Road that runs through the center of town. What is so urgent is known only to him and so far he's not seen fit to tell anyone.

Suicidal Woman

Perhaps, he trying to get help for another forlorn and less generous spirit that also inhabits the Inn at St. Peter's Village. There's a rumor that a young woman committed suicide on the 2nd floor of the Inn many years ago. Who she was in life is unknown, but her spirit has made it's presence known throughout the Inn and is most often spotted looking out one of the windows onto the rocks of the French Creek below the Inn. Perhaps she ended her young life by jumping out the window onto the rocks below. The owners and workers of the Inn have seen her often enough that they just take her existence as a fact of life...or maybe death.

Baby Cries

A third option for why Herbie's ghost might go seeking help in the village away from the Inn is the fact that a baby's disembodied crying has been heard. Ever since the 1940s, people who have stayed at the Inn and workers there have heard the sounds of a baby crying throughout the Inn, but they've never been able to find where it's coming from. There's no record of any infant deaths at the Inn and no one knows what to do about it, except perhaps Herbie.

St. Peter's Village is located in Chester County, Pennsylvania. It's just off Route 23 near Knauertown. Be careful; the small sign marking the entrance to St. Peter's Road is easy to miss if you blink.

ONE

Does John Brown's Spirit Haunt the Streets of Harper's Ferry?

Located on a small spit of land where the Potomac and Shenandoah Rivers converge, a visit to Harper's Ferry, West Virginia, is like stepping back to the nineteenth century. In 1859, a year before the start of the American Civil War, John Brown was waging a war of his own.

Be prepared to step back in time as you enter Harpers Ferry. *Courtesy of Cindy Wolf*

SECTION

John Brown was a very militant abolitionist. Not only did he feel that slavery was a sin, but in his mind, he felt that the only way that it could be wiped clean off of the country's soul was in a baptism of blood.

Brown's notion that slavery was evil wasn't a bad idea in itself. Many people were against the institution of slavery back then, both in the North and South of the Mason-Dixon line. But John Brown's method of ending slavery was definitely wrong, even among other abolitionists.

John Brown's master plan was to gather an army of militant abolitionists, then with this army free as many slaves as he could and arm them, so that they could rise up against their evil plantation overlords and in one fell swoop put an end to the evil slave states and eradicate the institution of slavery once and for all. A grand and bloody scheme indeed!

Why he chose Harper's Ferry of over more likely places to start his rebellion is a testament to John Brown's foolhardy lack of judgment when it came to planning. Instead of attacking further south where there were many cotton plantations filled with slaves, he instead chose to begin his military operation in the town of Harper's Ferry, where nearly half of the population were free men of color.

John Brown was bull-headed to say the least. He was warned by Harriet Tubman that she'd had a vision that he was walking into trap. One that he'd not escape. But Brown refused to change his plan to attack Harper's Ferry.

The prize this would-be hero of the slaves was after was two-fold: Brown wanted to gain control of the Federal Arsenal in order to supply his "army" with weapons. He also wanted control of the railroad station, because Harper's Ferry was a major junction. According to one of his sons, Salmon, Brown changed his mind over minor details of the raid almost constantly, but he wouldn't budge an inch on the overall plan to raid Harper's Ferry one bit. His main strategy was to seize control of the town, take as many hostages as possible and burn the town down if necessary to prove his resolve to the government that they meant business.

By a stroke if dumb luck, Brown's plan worked...or at least it did in the beginning. He and his eighteen followers, including his five sons, managed to sneak the five miles from their secret hideout, the Kennedy Farmhouse, into Harper's Ferry without being caught by the authorities. Ironically, the only casualty at this point was a man from Harper's Ferry who was a sympathizer to Brown's cause.

ONE

A free black man by the name of Haywood Shepherd or Shepherd Harwood (reports vary), who was a baggage man for the railroad, stumbled across the raiding party on their way into town. He had actually befriended some of the raiders earlier on some of their scouting visits to the town. He had surprised the raiders and they fired on him without realizing who he was, killing him on the spot.

As the ragtag raiders made their way under the cover of darkness into Harper's Ferry, they took several prisoners along the way. One of these captives was the great-grandnephew of our first president George Washington, Col. Lewis Washington.

It was at about this stage of the operation that things started to sour for the raiders. Instead of being greeted by throngs of grateful slaves, they were beset by a mob of angry, white townsfolk and were forced to retreat and barricade themselves in the small, brick building used by the arsenal as a fire engine house. This building would later be known as John Brown's Fort.

Brown and his followers were trapped, but they still refused to give up. Surrounded by the citizens of Harper's Ferry and the approaching Federal Troops, they still managed to kill Col. Beckham, the Mayor of Harper's Ferry.

The next morning, government forces led by none other than Robert E. Lee, arrived on the scene and wasted no time in attacking Brown's so-called fort. Lee's highly trained federal marines made quick work of capturing Brown's little army. It took them only three minutes to overpower the would-be liberators of slavery.

John Brown and his followers were given a trial. How fair a trial is up to debate. Most people knew what the outcome would be and weren't the least bit surprised when he was sentenced to death.

True to his nature as charismatic leader, Brown turned the trial into a platform extolling the shame of slavery and, for a brief time, he did manage to get world attention to his cause.

As he was led to the gallows to be hung for his crimes, John Brown handed a note to a nearby observer which read:

> I, John Brown, am now quite certain that the crimes of the guilty land will never be purged away but with blood. I had as I now think: vainly flattered myself that without very much bloodshed it might be done.

SECTION 2

John Brown's so called "Fort" where he and his followers took refuge. *Courtesy of Cindy Wolf*

Now, over a hundred years later, it seems as though the restless spirit of John Brown is still walking the streets of Harper's Ferry.

But why? Perhaps John Brown is still wandering the streets because he feels that he has unfinished business with the town. Regardless of why his spirit has decided to appear in Harper's Ferry, there are many stories of him making his presence known around the town.

Take for example: One of the most often repeated stories is of a man with a large black dog (John Brown had a black dog), who greatly resembles John Brown, so much so that tourists mistake him for a historical re-enactor who's playing the part of John Brown. As the man and his dog walk through the streets, people want to have their picture taken with him and he usually complies. But here's the strange and chilling part: In every case, when the people get those pictures developed there's one person missing from the photo. You guessed it: The supposed John Brown re-enactor!

ONE

Some tourists will even stop by the visitor's center and congratulate the person working the counter on how realistic the John Brown re-enactor looks and sounds, only to find out that there is no one scheduled that day to be portraying the would-be liberator.

Dangerfield Nubie

John Brown's spirit isn't the only one lurking around the streets of Harper' Ferry. Hog Alley, which cuts between Potomac and High Streets has a ghost of it's own: A free black man with the unusual name of Dangerfield Nubie. Dangerfield was part of John Brown's raiding party who had a last minute change of heart about the success of their mission and decided that retreat would be the better part of valor. He tried to slip out of the Engine-House-turned-fort, but was shot by a group of angry citizens of Harper' Ferry and killed instantly. To add insult to injury, the unruly mob of angry citizens proceeded to mutilate Nubie's body after his death.

Some people have spotted John Brown's spirit along this street.
Courtesy of Cindy Wolf

SECTION

It's poor Nubie's spirit that has been spotted walking in Hog Alley late at night by residents and park employees. They often mistake him for just another late night stroller, that is until he disappears before their eyes!

Some of the civil war re-enactors may be more than meets the eye on the streets of Harpers Ferry. *Courtesy of Cindy Wolf*

ONE

Cindy and I made our first trip to Harper's Ferry a few years ago. As much of a Civil War buff that I am, I had never been to Harper's Ferry and neither had she. We had heard that it was haunted and were looking forward to going on at least one ghost tour, but unfortunately the weather was not cooperating the day we decided to visit the town.

The weather for most of the day was pleasant, even though it was overcast. As our luck held out, there was a group of Civil War re-enactors in the town that day which greatly helped add to the overall feeling for the history of the town.

We walked the cobblestone streets and tried to keep an eye out for anything out of the ordinary, but we never saw anyone resembling John Brown or his black dog. We even went to the Engine House that served as his makeshift fort during the raid, but there was no feeling of the paranormal. That could have been due to the fact that there were dozens of other people there at the same time.

Hog Alley had a definite eerie feel to it, maybe because it is tucked out of the way of the main streets, but it did have a creepy vibe to it. Although we still didn't get any paranormal photos or any other evidence, it was easy to see how at night it would be very secluded.

Overall, Harper's Ferry is a fascinating place to visit. It is very much like stepping back in time and I'm sure at nighttime it's even more so. If you find your way there, I'm sure that Ghost Tours of Harper's Ferry will be happy to accommodate you for a tour, and who knows, you might be lucky enough to be guided by old John B. himself.

> Harper's Ferry is located in Jefferson County, West Virginia. It sits at a confluence of two rivers, The Potomac and the Shenandoah. Three states converge there as well, Maryland, Virginia, and West Virginia. The lower section of the town is located inside the Harper's Ferry National Historic site.

SECTION

Railroad

TWO

Aside from sailors, I can't think of another means of travel or travel occupation that has more legends and hauntings associated with it than the railroads. Spectral locomotives, headless linemen and all sorts of haunted railroad crossings exist all over the world. From Abe Lincoln's ghostly funeral train to various tragic railroad workers such as Joe Baldwin, there's no shortage tales of ghost lights, tragic train accidents repeating time and time again, and cursed locomotives.

Railroads have a long history of hauntings.
Courtesy of Cindy Wolf

Wraiths

Does Big John Still Haunt the Big Bend Tunnel?

Eleven miles east of Hinton, West Virginia, stands Big Bend Mountain. Inside this mountain is a mile-long tunnel that stands as a testament to the ultimate *Man versus Machine* battle of the late nineteenth century, and it has left behind a ghostly legend in American Folklore as well as notoriety in many different books, songs, and movies.

Big John Henry was born a slave in the 1840s in Missouri. Exactly where, no one is certain. But what they are certain is that he was a big infant weighing in at a whopping thirty-three pounds, and if you believe the legend, not only was he a large child, but he was supposed to have been born with a hammer in his hand.

By all accounts, he grew into a big man as well. Six foot tall and 200 pounds of pure muscle. Naturally, he turned his God-given strength to good use. After the Civil War, he was freed from slavery and began a career working for the railroad as a steel driver.

Big John, as he was called, was in his mid thirties around 1870 when his greatest challenge presented itself. A challenge that was to make him an American folk hero for all time. He was working for the Chesapeake & Ohio Railroad as a steel driver when the railroad owners unveiled a machine called the Burleigh Steam-Powered Drill.

The railroad Big John Worked for, The Chesapeake & Ohio Railroad, started out as the Louisa Railroad of Louisa County, Virginia, in 1836, and as an even earlier incarnation, the James River & Kanawha Canal Company in 1785.

In 1850, a mere ten years or so before the outbreak of Civil War, after several mergers with other minor railroad lines, it was renamed the "Virginia Central Railway."

During the Civil War, the Virginia Central Railroad was very important to the fledgling Confederacy. It, like many other railroads, was used to transport food and other supplies from the Shenandoah Valley to the Confederate capital, Richmond, Virginia. Not only did the railroad transport food, but it was also used to transport troops to the various battlefields.

After the end of the Civil War, the Virginia Central Railroad was all but bankrupt. They managed to convince a railroad mogul in New York named Collis P. Huntington to invest in the railroad, thus saving it from extinction.

Huntington, one of the big four railroad owners involved in the transcontinental railroad, merged the Virginia Central line with his Ohio Railroad and on July 1, 1867, the railroad was renamed once again – this time as the Chesapeake & Ohio Railroad.

After, there were many different mergers with other railroads, such as the B & O, Western Maryland, and the Atlantic Coast Line and others. Now, many decades later, CSX is today one of only four major railroads left in America.

But back in 1870, the C & O Railroad still had much expanding to do. To help with this, the owners bought a revolutionary new piece of equipment that would help speed work in tunneling through mountains. A very slow and time-consuming job. This is why they bought the Burleigh Steam-Powered Drill. To the steel drivers, like Big John Henry, this contraption might as well have been the devil. Its existence threatened their very livelihood.

Charles Burleigh had a falling out with his partners in developing a steam-powered drill. He refined the design of the steam drill they had been working on by himself, and just to make sure there were no later legal battles, he bought the Fowle drill patent. (Burleigh had helped build the original Couch/Fowle drill while employed as a machinist in Fitchburg, Massachusetts) Eerily, it was placed into service on October 31, 1866 (I wonder if there was a full moon...). This steam drill was also used on the Hoosic Tunnel in Massachusetts which has several ghost stories associated with it as well.

According to American folklore, Big John Henry was a formidable former slave who was employed by the C & O Railroad, as I've said, as a steel driver. Over the years, he gained the reputation as the "greatest" steel driver in the world. With the aid of his mighty hammer, Big John helped the railroad expand westward, but one day in 1870, when the railroad owner bought the steam-powered hammer/drill, the human steel drivers were to be replaced – including Big John.

Outraged, Big John challenged the railroad owner to a contest: *Man versus Machine*, winner take all! Big Bend Mountain in Talcott, West Virginia, was chosen as the site of the contest. (Several researchers dispute this, but so far there has been no solid evidence to prove otherwise.)

SECTION

Big John Henry, with a huge twenty-pound hammer in each hand, furiously started pounding away alongside the steam-powered hammer, and in the end, after a grueling struggle of endurance and skill, Big John triumphed over the machine – but at a fatal cost. Just after being declared the winner, as his fellow steel drivers were congratulating him, Big John fell to the ground dead!

It seems that as strong as he was, he succumbed to a very small killer. A blood vessel burst in his head and he died of a massive stroke! So ended the life of John Henry and began the Folklore and legends.

To this day the citizens of Talcott, still honor his achievements by holding a three-day celebration each year called "John Henry Days."

As for the paranormal part of this story: They say that on certain nights, if you go into Big Bend Tunnel and are very still and quiet, you can still hear the sound of Big John's hammering echo throughout the tunnel.

Talcott, West Virginia is located in Summers County. It's situated along West Virginia Route 3 and the Greenbrier River on the east side of Hinton, West Virginia. Big Bend Tunnel is a mile-long tunnel that cuts through the Big Bend Mountain, which is on Highway 12.

TWO

Abraham Lincoln's Funeral Train
(New York Central Railroad Tracks)

There are few events that will unite our country. Most of these are of a tragic nature on a grand scale rather than a happy event. Recently, it has been 9/11, the destruction of the World Trade Center, the Pentagon, and Flight 93.

In the twentieth century, some of the tragedies were World War 1, World War 2, and the assassination of President John F. Kennedy.

Back in the nineteenth century, the citizens of America had to endure two tragedies back-to-back: The Civil War and the brutal assassination of the great emancipator, President Abraham Lincoln.

When Lincoln's death was announced to the public, there was a national mass mourning. In order to appease the public and add closure to the tragic event, the coffin and Lincoln's body were placed in reverence on a special funeral train. This special train was boarded by a special group of 300 honor guard soldiers and a military concert band who played music while onlookers paid their respects.

Ever since that day, various people have spotted what appears to be a ghostly apparition of the funeral train on the anniversary of its sad journey.

The phantom train starts its fateful journey in Washington, D.C. and then proceeds to New York State before heading out towards Springfield, Illinois. Sadly, it never actually makes it there and is doomed to repeat this for all eternity.

Although many people have spotted this ghostly train in various locations along it's original route (some of the areas no longer even have tracks), they have almost unanimously described the same encounter.

According to many different witnesses, the first thing they notice is a strange, unearthly blue light that tips them off they are witnessing something not of this world. Some people claim that for the duration of the train's passing, which usually takes six minutes, there will be an eerie silence as if the tracks were covered with some sort of noise-canceling carpet. Yet other people claim to hear the sound of a lone, old-fashioned steam whistle blowing a mournful blast.

Regardless of what people hear, most witness have all seen the exact same thing. They generally see an old-fashioned steam engine complete with a shiny brass smokestack pulling two railroad cars. These railroad cars and the engine pulling them are draped in black cloth as if involved with a mourning trip.

If, at first, witnesses were unsure they were seeing something paranormal pass in front of them, the next scene would confirm it for them. What comes next is the engine being tended by not a flesh and blood crew but a literal skeleton crew, and directly following behind them is a band made up of skeletal musicians in the next car playing haunting funeral music as they pass.

The next, and last car, is filled with blue uniformed federal soldiers guarding a coffin, believed to be President Lincoln's resting place. Some of these soldiers have coffins strapped to their own backs although why this is no one is exactly sure.

One interesting fact that isn't really paranormal, but is weird just the same, is that Lincoln's Funeral Train traveled exactly 1,700 miles from Washington, D.C. to Springfield, Illinois. And 1,700 days is exactly how long the Civil War lasted. I thought this was sort of ironic...

So, if you ever have to travel at the end of April and you're in the states of New York, Pennsylvania, or Maryland, and you have to stop at a rural railroad crossing at night. Keep your eyes peeled. You might just see more than meets the eye.

The Haunted Tracks of the Yukon and White Pass Railroad

During a recent trip to Alaska on Norwegian Cruise Lines, Cindy and I had a chance to take a train ride on the famous White Pass and Yukon Route train. Our ship, the *Norwegian Pearl* made port on the historic town of Skagway and we were disembarked to catch our train.

The White Pass and Yukon Railroad has at least two spirits haunting its winding tracks. *Courtesy of Cindy Wolf*

The town of Skagway is very small the streets are still much as they were back in the 1800s. Most, if not all, of the buildings still have a look and feel of that time period. You almost expect to see the spirit of some miner come walking out of one the stores on the main street.

Skagway has a long history of habitation dating back to prehistoric times. Although it wasn't called Skagway back then. In the native Tlingit, it was called Skagua, which means *windy place* and if you've ever been there, you'll agree that the name fits. Even at the end of August, you'll want to wear a light windbreaker because of the cool air and breeze.

SECTION

Jumping ahead several hundred years, the town of Skagua officially had its named changed to Skagway in 1898. This was a booming time for the town in more ways than one. The year 1898 marked the start of the Alaskan Gold Rush and the population of the town swelled to 8,000 to 10,000 people almost overnight. More importantly, at least to this book, was the starting of the construction of the White Pass and Yukon Railroad. Looking at the small town of Skagway today, I can hardly believe that 10,000 people could've lived there at one time.

By the year 1900, things had died down quite a bit. The Gold Rush boom had fizzled out and there were only about 3,117 people living in the town then. The good news was that the White Pass and Yukon Railroad had been completed in record time. To commemorate the occasion, a golden spike was hammered in on July, 29th at Carcross, Yukon.

During our trip, this was the first time either us had ever been to Skagway (or Alaska, for that matter), and of course I had to go and ask about any local hauntings. (I can't help it. It's just my nature.) I started asking at the Visitors' Center on Main Street and was told that there were two places in town that were supposed to be haunted. The Red Onion Saloon and Golden North Hotel both harbored spirits. I did look into both places, but since neither of them had anything to do with the subject of this particular book, I had to shelve the investigation for another time. However, the employee at the Visitors' Center did mention that along the route of the White Pass and Yukon Railroad tracks there were supposed to be some haunted spots, and that if I asked when we were aboard the train, they assured me the tour guide could point them out. Now, I was getting some where.

When you go on a cruise, there's always time to look around the port you're in and that's just what Cindy and I did while we waited for our excursion on the train to begin. To be sure, I wanted a chance to look at the haunted spots over in the town as much as possible while Cindy just plain wanted to shop.

Soon it was time to board the tour bus that would take us to our starting point in the little town of Carcross, Yukon. This was actually the mid point on the railway. We boarded the Victorian-looking steam engine here to start our sixty-seven and a half mile trek back to the town of Skagway. Even in the summer, which is when we were there, you still wanted to use a coat as it was a bit cold.

Riding on the White Pass and Yukon Railroad is an amazing experience. The scenery cannot be duplicated anywhere else in the world. Just sight

TWO

of these humongous mountains covered in clouds and to smell the crisp clean air is worth the price. If you think that this is just a normal railroad ride, though, forget it.

Just building this rail line was an amazing task. These men built a narrow gage railroad through some of the highest mountainous terrain in the world. Blasting through these coastal mountains is tough enough, but they did it in a quick twenty-six months and this was back in the 1800s! Just to put things into perspective, they had to lay 110 miles of track, blast their way through two mountains, and build numerous bridges and trestles to accommodate the trains. Where I live, it took the Pennsylvania Department of Transportation four years just to rebuild a small two-lane bridge that wasn't even a quarter of a mile across.

The WP&YR is an International Historic Civil Engineering Landmark that ranks with other huge structures such as, the Panama Canal, the Eiffel Tower, and the Statue of Liberty. To build this railroad through the mountains, it took a whopping 450 tons of explosives. You can guess that with that sheer amount of firepower, there were bound to be an accident or two – and right you are!

Although the landscape is beautiful, these tracks were difficult and deadly to run up the mountains outside of Skagway, Alaska.
Courtesy of Cindy Wolf

As we came out of the second tunnel of the train ride, our guide directed us to look at a large boulder that was just off the tracks. She explained that the boulder was part of a misfiring of explosives that dislodged the boulder and ended up crushing two railroad workers, killing them instantly on the spot and that they couldn't even move the massive boulder to recover their bodies. They are under the boulder to this day.

Sometimes, she said, engineers working the trains at night would spot their spirits either standing on the tracks or on top of the boulder.

This photo, taken on the moving train, is where the spirits of two men who were killed while building the rail line manifest most often. This falling boulder was their demise and marks their grave. *Courtesy of Cindy Wolf*

While the train chugged along the tracks, I kept seeing a stone trail that ran almost parallel to the tracks and every so often you would see a sign that read: TRAIL OF 98'. I asked about the trail and the guide said that the Trail of 98' was what the prospectors who were searching for gold had to use to get to the gold mines in the Yukon since the railroad hadn't been built as of that time. Thousands of people used that trail in just two years time. Many would-be prospectors and their mules died while traveling along that trail. Sometimes at night, the spirits of those miners and even their mules and pack horses have be seen walking the Trail of 98' still searching for that elusive mother lode of gold.

The White Pass and Yukon railroad officially shut down as a mining train in 1982. But in 1988, it was reopened as a tourist attraction and served about 37,000 tourists that first season. Nowadays, it's such a popular excursion that 450,000 people ride on it each season. Who knows; with that many people riding this train, hopefully somebody will take notice of a spirit or two of those hardy prospectors.

The White Pass and Yukon Railway runs from Skagway, Alaska to Carcross, Yukon Territory. Generally trips are one way depending on what day of the week you arrive. After your train ride, you take a bus back to your starting point.

TWO

Specters of the Strasburg Railroad

To be honest, when I initially came up with the idea for this book, the Strasburg Railroad was one of the first places I thought of investigating, but in reality it became one of the last places that I looked into for the paranormal. I changed my mind when I was at a book signing last Halloween at Blockbuster Video in Bridgeport, Pennsylvania.

This is one of the first orbs that Cindy captured on film. It was taken on the Strasburg Railroad the day after our wedding. *Courtesy of Cindy Wolf*

As I was signing books and talking to people about various paranormal subjects, a couple came up and we chatted about the different books I had written and I mentioned I was writing this book about haunted travel. The woman of the couple, asked if I had ever been to the Strasburg Railroad and if I was going to write about it in this volume. I answered, "Well, I've been to the railroad, but I don't really have too much research about any hauntings there. If I do hear anything I'd be glad to put it in the book."

She replied, "Well, we were there and when we took some pictures we had some orbs show up. One was in a passenger car and the other was outside the train." She continued, "But the one, outside the train showed up as a blue orb and the one inside the train was white."

Cindy looked over at me and said in amazement, "You have got to be kidding!" Then she turned and looked at the woman. "We have similar picture's from the Strasburg Railroad." Then she added, "But, we took ours four years ago. We went to the Strasburg Railroad for a day trip, the day after our wedding."

"True. We did," I added, nodding in agreement. I thought to myself, looks like I'm going to be adding a chapter on the Strasburg Railroad to the book after all.

I've lived all my life in Lancaster County and my Uncle Bill even lived in Strasburg for several decades, so I'd visited the town quite a bit growing up. My grandfather was a huge model train buff and he would always want to ride the Strasburg Railroad every chance he got. I think that I was so used to being in Strasburg that I just took the whole railroad gig for granted and never really appreciated it as I was growing up.

As I look at Strasburg from a paranormal Investigator's view, I had to ask myself: What was it about Strasburg that seemed to draw paranormal energy to the place? Besides the obvious tourist draw of the Railroad, The Pennsylvania Railroad Museum, and the fact that it's in the heart of Pennsylvania Dutch country, there are also not one, but two walking ghost tours from different companies. I now hear the Strasburg Railroad itself has a walking ghost tour that visits several spots in the railroad station. They have almost as many ghost tours as Gettysburg! I was pretty sure that Strasburg wasn't as haunted as Gettysburg, but who knows? Something had to be drawing people there.

The Borough of Strasburg has been in existence since the 1700s, although it wasn't always called Strasburg. Originally, there were a lot of "poor houses" and the name of "Begger Town" was given to the area. Supposedly, at least a few people used to call the town "Hell's Hole," but safe to say that never caught on.

The Strasburg Railroad itself was founded in 1832 and used mostly to carry freight but it did also accommodate passengers. The railroad was almost shut down for good in 1957 due to storms damaging the tracks, but it was revived and has the distinction of being the oldest short-line railroad in America.

Strasburg is on the National Registry of Historic Places and really deserves to be on a national registry of haunted places. Legend has it that you can sometimes see a covered wagon or carriage (ghostly, of course) rolling down Main Street in Strasburg with a load of drunken,

TWO

Is this railroad station house haunted by the spirit of Mrs. Humboldt? *Courtesy of Cindy Wolf*

---

whooping and hollering Civil War soldiers who were on leave and traveling through town. Why this occurs no one really knows. Perhaps they were so drunk that they crashed their wagon and are now doomed to repeat their neverending leave of absence. Or, maybe they just had such a good time, they like to return at repeat the fun.

Mr. Billingsly

According to Theresa Summers, the tour guide of the Strasburg Railroad Ghost Walk tours, there are several spirits that haunt the little railroad station. One of these is a man by the name of John Billingsly. Mr. Billingsly was a great fan of steam engines and evidently couldn't spend enough time riding on them. Supposedly, he was either riding in a steam engine or was inspecting one in 1972 when hurricane Agnes hit the area, causing massive flooding and destruction. Hurricane Agnes was one of the worst storms to hit Lancaster County. (My paternal grandparents lost their home when Muddy Run Creek overflowed.)

Apparently, Mr. Billingsly sought refuge in Engine 89 and was drowned when it flooded. Rumor had it that he liked the engine so much that he decided to make it his permanent place of residence in the afterlife.

The Station House

The next spirit that Ms. Summer's talks about is in the railroad station itself. Originally, the station house was in East Petersburg, Pennsylvania, in the 1920s and was moved to its present location. At the time that it was in East Pete, (as we Lancastrians call it), it was run by a man named Humboldt. Mrs. Humboldt fell in love with another railroad man, named Arthur, but he was unaware of Mrs. Humboldt's affection – or chose to ignore it. Sadly, Mr. Humboldt believed that there was an actual real extramarital affair going on and took matters into his own hands.

Being the Stationmaster, Mr. Humboldt held a position of power in town and he contacted his friend the Mayor, and between the two of them, they managed to frame Arthur for burglary and vandalism. Arthur was sent directly to jail. Poor Arthur never did get a trial, because before he was to have his day in court, he was found dead in his cell, where it was assumed he committed suicide, by hanging himself.

But, the big question remains: Did he really kill himself or did Mr. Humboldt have a hand in his death. Nothing to link Humboldt to Arthur's death was ever found, but I suspect that Mrs. Humboldt might have suspected as much also.

TWO

Even thought Mrs. Humboldt had her doubts about her husband's innocence in Arthur's death, she still stayed with him. She too would later die under mysterious circumstances. But it was only when the train station was moved to its current location in Strasburg, did things truly come to light. It seems a body, (little more than bones) was found in the station and they were identified as Mrs. Humboldt's remains. Remains, I might add, that showed her death was not a natural one. No one knows how exactly her body was placed there or the circumstances of her demise. But, her spirit has been seen haunting the station ever since her earthly remains were discovered.

So, is the Strasburg Railroad haunted? It would seem so. Cindy and I really weren't searching for ghosts on the day we captured the Orbs at the railroad, but then you never know when you'll have an encounter with the supernatural.

The Strasburg Railroad is located on Route 741, 1 ½ miles east of Strasburg's center square in Lancaster County, Pennsylvania. The train runs on a short line round-trip between Strasburg, Pennsylvania and Paradise, Pennsylvania.

SECTION

Cursed Cars

THREE

To be perfectly clear, there are two types of Phantom Vehicles. On the one hand you have the rather mundane type of phantom vehicle that insurance companies call any vehicle that causes damage to a vehicle that they're insuring even though there is no physical contact between them. In this book, however, we are only interested in the second type of phantom vehicle.

These types of phantom vehicles are paranormal in nature. A typical, as much as a paranormal encounter can be called typical, encounter with one of these phantom vehicles is that the ghostly car or truck will appear quickly out of nowhere and to the observer may seem to be without a driver or sometimes is seen being driven by the ghost of the former deceased owner. An example of this would be the ghost of Peter Rugg and his daughter who drive a ghostly horse-drawn carriage throughout New England, eternally searching for their home in Boston.

All over the world there have been sightings of these vehicles and they usually take place on rural back roads or empty highways, but you never know... That driver that just cut in front of you might be traveling a bit farther than you think.

and Phantom Vehicles

SECTION

The Crazed Driver

Highways are dangerous places. Thousands of people get injured or killed on our nation's highways each year and yet we still use them to get from one destination to another. Highway 4 between Orlando, Florida, and Daytona is a major highway and is haunted not by any particular human phantom, but a phantom car.

This phantom car isn't alone. It has a counterpart phantom eighteen-wheeler truck that haunts Highway 4 near Tampa, Florida, and between the two of them, I'm sure they've racked up a number of late-night accidents on this stretch of road.

No one knows when the phantom car first made its appearance on the Orlando/Daytona Highway, but it's well documented as to what it does: It causes accidents. The phantom car will typically appear out of thin air at night along Highway 4 and weave erratically in and out of traffic at a high speed, and get this: Whatever entity is driving this spectral vehicle, it does so without headlights. It's bad enough when real-live drivers do this at night, but a phantom car has nothing to lose. What's it gonna do — crash?

An erratically driven ghost car has been spotted on this stretch of highway in Florida.

At least the phantom truck is a bit more responsible. Since 1985 this ghostly semi has been seen following trucks hauling produce. At least two sightings of the Phantom Truck have occurred on Highway 4 twelve miles east of Tampa.

The one and only time Cindy and I have been on Highway 4, we were held up in traffic because of an accident in the eastbound direction as we were heading from Orlando to Daytona. I didn't spot any phantom cars, but the one that was involved in the accident was very mangled. (One never knows...)

THREE

The Little Bastard– James Dean's Death Car

Live fast. Die young. That was James Dean's legacy. Born on February 8th, 1931, James Dean epitomized the word *cool*. Even though he only made three movies, with his most famous being *Rebel Without a Cause*, he became a Hollywood screen legend after crashing his car, "The Little Bastard," on December 30th, 1955. The events of that tragic day would give birth to a mystery that exists even to this day.

The day started out normal enough. James Dean was a car racing enthusiast and liked to drive fast. Dean and his mechanic, Rolf Wutherich, were traveling along a state route towards the west near Cholame, California, going to a car race in Salinas, California. Dean was driving, and some people claim that he was speeding, but after examining the accident site, it was reported that he couldn't have been going any faster than 55 mile an hour.

I'm sure they were having a pleasant drive and talking about the upcoming race and how well they thought the new car they were driving, the Porsche Spyder, would perform. Originally, they were going to tow the car behind Dean's station wagon, but Dean decided against that because he wanted more time behind the wheel of the Porsche to see how well it handled and he also wanted to get more familiar with driving it himself.

At this same time, coming from the opposite direction, was a twenty-three-year-old college student named Donald Turnupseed. Little did he know that his name would be connected forever with James Dean's legacy. Turnupseed was driving along State Route 41 in his 1950 Ford Custom Tudor Coupe. As Donald Turnupseed reached the intersection of State Route 41 and State Road 46 he was unable to see James Dean making the same turn from the opposite direction and they both collided in a head-on collision.

Looking at both vehicles, it's easy to see who would have had the greater chance of surviving the crash. The Ford was almost twice the size of Dean's Porsche Spyder. Turnupseed's car was built like a tank and must have easily outweighed Dean's "Little Bastard." Add to the fact, that the Spyder was an open-top racing car that sat very low to the ground compared to the Ford, and you could almost feel the bone crunching jarring that Dean would feel as his head made contact with the front grill of the Ford.

What is kind of weird is that James Dean was warned by none other than Alec Guinness, old Obi Wan Kenobi of *Star Wars*, that the Porsche would be the death of him. Dean met Alec Guinness outside of a restaurant and showed off the "Little Bastard" to him, and his first impression was that the car looked sinister. He told Dean, "If you get in that car, you will be found dead in it by this time next week." Perhaps Alec was channeling "The Force" when he made this prediction, because seven days later, that's exactly what happened.

James Dean was unconscious and severely injured, but still breathing when he was taken by ambulance to Paso Robles War Memorial Hospital. According to hospital records, he died at 5:59 P.M. on September 30, 1955.

As for the people involved in James Dean's accident, mechanic Rolf was thrown from the Porsche Spyder and suffered a broken jaw or leg (reports vary) and other serious head injuries, but lived.

Don Turnupseed, the driver of the Ford Tudor, came out of the accident in much better shape. He only had a gashed forehead and a bruised nose.

The Porsche Spyder 550, that was totaled in the accident, was bought for parts by two other racing enthusiasts – doctors by the names of Troy McHenry and William Eschrid. This is where the curse of the "Little Bastard" took off in full force.

Dr. McHenry took the engine from Dean's Spyder and used it in his own race car. During a race in which he and Dr. Eschrid were both competing, his car spun out of control and he crashed into a tree – he died upon impact.

In the same race, Dr. Eschrid was seriously injured when his car rolled over while he was making a turn on a curve.

Now before this race, the doctors sold the mangled chassis of Dean's car to George Barris for $2,500. George Barris was a car customizer who, later in his life, designed the "Batmobile" used on the *Batman* TV series starring Adam West in the 60s.

Trouble seemed to follow the "Little Bastard" wherever it went. While taking the wreck off the trailer, it slipped and broke both legs

THREE

of the mechanic. Barris sold two of the tires to a young kid who used them on his car. As far as anyone knew, the tires were in perfect shape as they suffered no damage in the crash. But, while the new owner was driving his car with the tires on it, he lost control of the vehicle when both of the tires inexplicably exploded at the same time.

With the "Little Bastard" being so famous as the car James Dean died in, it was inevitable that some one would try to steal a souvenir off of it. One would-be thief got a nasty cut on his arm from a jagged piece of metal when he tried to steal the steering wheel. Another thief, at a different place and time, tried to steal the bloodstained driver's seat and was also injured for his trouble.

Finally deciding that the car was too much trouble, Barris donated it as a display on driving safety to the California Highway Patrol. Even in the hands of law enforcement the curse of the "Little Bastard" would not be calmed.

The second time they set up the car to display at Sacramento High School, the mangled car slipped off a truck and broke a students hip. This would continue to be a bad habit with this car. It almost seems like the car would jump off and purposely attack people at random. It almost sounds like a plot of a Stephen King novel.

Still, the car seems to have a charmed life. Even fire couldn't damage it. The C.H.P. had a garage where they stored it when it wasn't on display, and while the car was there, the garage caught fire. Everything was destroyed except...the Porsche Spyder. It wasn't even scorched in the fire.

The "Little Bastard" just would not stay where it belonged. When it was being transported to Salinas, California, the truck transporting it lost control and the driver was ejected from the cab. To add insult to injury, the Porsche slipped off the bed of the truck, flipped over and crushed the already injured driver, killing him. The "Little Bastard" also slipped of a truck two other times while it was being transported.

All of these mishaps and accidents happened in a five-year period starting with the death of James Dean and ending in 1960. You see, there is one final mystery surrounding the Porsche Spyder: No one knows what ever happened to it. It was last seen on display in Miami, Florida, and was scheduled to go back to Los Angeles, but the "Little Bastard" in one last final act of defiance never arrived there. Somewhere it disappeared and it's been missing ever since.

SECTION

Ghostly sounds of screeching tires and crunching metal have been heard by drivers passing near a tree where James Dean had his fatal accident. The original accident site is now a pasture and the roads were realigned to make the intersection safer.

If you're interested in visiting the location, there's a James Dean Memorial that was dedicated in 1977 made out of concrete and steel. If you happen to see a Porsche Spyder 550 around the area, you might want to get out of the way, because who knows, it might just be James Dean and the "Little Bastard" attempting to complete their final journey.

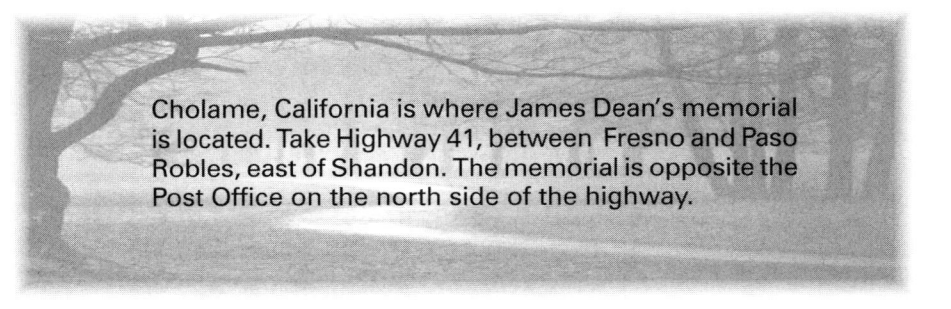

Cholame, California is where James Dean's memorial is located. Take Highway 41, between Fresno and Paso Robles, east of Shandon. The memorial is opposite the Post Office on the north side of the highway.

THREE

Phantom Stagecoaches

Before there was a transcontinental railroad and the invention of the automobile, weary travelers had to rely on a system of stagecoaches that would conceivably get you from the east coast or to the west. As trains took over the majority of mass travel, stagecoaches were phased out, much like the Pony Express. What they left behind, however, was a large number of stagecoach stops that would linger as a reminder of a bygone era. The stagecoaches using these stops may be gone, but they're not forgotten. Some refuse to fade away and the phantoms of this once-mighty system of transportation still make their presence known.

The Black Stagecoach

In Santa Ynez, northeast of Santa Barbara, California, on a narrow stretch of road that winds its way to Solvang, there have been reports of a phantom stagecoach that makes its ethereal rounds driven by four inky black horses and a lanky driver wearing a tall, black hat. It's not surprising to the locals. They've been seeing this trail-side phantom for over 100 years.

As recent as the late 1980s, drivers have spotted this black carriage, on Solvang Road and some other roads in the Santa Ynez area. A few drivers have also reported that the coach is sometimes illuminated by lanterns on either side of the carriage and inside the coach sits an old woman, unmoving as if she were a statue. Who she is and where she's going are still a question to this very day.

The Red Stagecoach

On the other side of the United States in Winchester, Virginia, a fiery, red phantom stagecoach has its origins from during the Civil War. Spying is a risky venture and no matter what time period the venture is taking place, every spy knows that they are expendable.

SECTION

That must have been going through the mind of a northern operative as he desperately tried to get a message to the Union Army about an impending attack by none other than Confederate General Stonewall Jackson.

The desperate man knew he had to make the attempt to contact the federal troops by any means necessary, so on May 24, 1862, he hijacked the Shenandoah stagecoach in hopes that he could reach them in time. As he made his getaway, the Confederate army was hot on his heels, but he had a decent lead on his way to Winchester to inform Major General Nathaniel Banks of the attack.

Unfortunately, the weather was not cooperating, and as the speeding stagecoach approached the crossroads at Mt. Jackson, it was struck by a bolt of lightning. The Union spy was flash fried in his seat and died on the spot.

One of the weird bits of information I ran across while searching this story was that on the same day, May 24, 1862, *Harper's Weekly*, a popular magazine from the nineteenth century, ran a political cartoon illustrating Confederate President Jefferson Davis riding in a coach driven by a skeleton wearing a top hat with the caption: "Jeff Davis's New Coachman (his Old One having come over to McDowell) driving him in the direction of the LAST DITCH." Now, from what I can gather at this point, whoever drew the cartoon was trying to say that the Confederacy was making one last ditch effort to win the war. The fact was, at this time, the Confederacy was actually doing better than the Union Army and was just on the verge of winning the Battle of Winchester. Not that this has much to do with the Phantom Stagecoach, but I thought it was ironic that this cartoon had the skeleton driver on the day that the Union Spy had been struck by lightening.

Nowadays, drivers along U.S. Highway 11 are witnesses to a ghostly coach painted in fire engine red that kicks up a supernatural amount of dust as it passes them by towards Winchester. Some witnesses have claimed to see the blackened, charred remains of the unfortunate Union spy sitting in the drivers seat guiding the four white horses that power the coach on his endless quest to reach the Union Army.

THREE

The Vallecito Station and The Carrizo Wash Station

In 1857, Butterfield Mail Company established a stagecoach route from St. Louis, Missouri, to San Francisco, California. Sure it would get you there in twenty-four hours, but the trip was so harsh, that travelers nicknamed it the Journey of Death, and for some people, it really was the death of them. At least two stagecoach stops along this route are considered to be very haunted: The Vallecito Station and The Carrizo Wash Station.

Located in Anza Barrego State Park, the Carrizo Wash has had sightings of a phantom stagecoach that is supposed to be a sort of *Flying Dutchman* of the desert.

The origin of this *Flying Dutchman* of the desert starts in 1860. It seems that a stagecoach from El Paso, Texas, was on its way to San Diego, California, with a gold shipment. You'd think that it would be well protected, but such was not the case. Either the owners weren't afraid the coach would be robbed or they were just plain stupid because all they sent for protection was one guard. Even nowadays Brinks trucks have more than one guard protecting the money.

To make matters even worse, the one guard became ill in Yuma and stayed behind to recover while the stagecoach continued on to San Diego with only a driver and no protection. Sure enough, not too much further along the trail, the stagecoach was held-up at gunpoint. Somehow, whether it was just bad luck or the bandits were afraid they'd be followed, they shot the poor driver through the heart, and as he slumped dead over the reins, the four-mule team got spooked by the sound of gunfire and ran off into the desert taking the coach and the dead driver into oblivion. The coach was never seen again, or I should say the corporeal, solid coach was never seen again, because plenty of people have not only seen but heard the phantom version of the stagecoach.

Campers and Park Rangers from between Carrizo Wash and Agua Caliente have reported hearing the sounds of a runaway stagecoach running throughout the desert at night and then the next morning they'll find odd, unexplained wheel ruts in the sand as if a coach had passed through the area. Occasionally, someone will claim to have seen an old stagecoach with only a lone driver and no passengers on the old Butterfield road.

SECTION

Also located in the confines of the Anza Barrego State Park is an old Stagecoach stop called Vallecito Station. It may no longer be an active stagecoach stop, but with several spirits haunting the small adobe building, it's a very active paranormal location.

The station was opened in 1853 as a stop on the Butterfield Stagecoach route and was in use only until 1888, but in that short period of time it's managed to conjure up quite a diverse contingent of supernatural phenomena. The Vallecito Station was re-opened in 1934 as a historic site and people have been eager to visit, not just because of the paranormal, but it's also a nice place to go camping.

The spirits that call the station home are very diverse. There's a ghostly white horse that hangs about the outside of the station. Then there's the most famous spirit: The Lady in White. And although they're not the most famous spirits, they are the most playful: good ol' cowpokes, Buck and Randall, will more than likely make their presence known to people camping out at night at the station.

In the 1850s a young woman named, Eileen O' Connor undertook the rough stagecoach journey from St. Louis, Missouri, to Sacramento, California, to marry her wealthy fiancé. She was frail in health to begin with and the harsh travel didn't help her condition. While she was in Yuma, (What is it with Yuma and people getting ill?), she contracted some kind of illness and by the time she reached Vallecito Station, she was deathly ill. Too weak to move, she insisted that it was only exhaustion from the journey and that in a few days she'd catch the next stage. She never did leave on any stage. Poor Miss O'Connor died from exhaustion that very night.

After searching her meager bags, they found a hand-made white wedding dress and since it was the nicest clothes she had, they buried her in it at the nearby cemetery.

Years later, after the station had closed and then became a historic site, campers and Park Rangers started seeing the apparition of a young woman in a long white dress drifting and floating around the Vallecito Station. One can only presume that it's the restless spirit of Eileen O'Connor. Sometimes her spirit is seen at twilight floating up out of the dusty ground from her grave. She then proceeds to float over to the front of the station and then linger there, hanging in midair as if she were waiting for the next coach to take her to final destination, little realizing that she's already there.

THREE

A very brave or foolhardy man who saw her forlorn spirit claimed to have actually reached out and touched her and received an electric shock for his audacity.

Park workers who were digging a foundation for a new restroom facility encountered her spirit hovering over them as they were digging out the hole for the plumbing. Overall, the Lady in White is one of the more recognizable spirits in the area, but she's not the only one.

The ghostly form of a white horse is supposedly the former mount of a bandit who was shot by his former partners after they buried the loot from a stagecoach robbery. So much for honor among thieves (I guess they didn't feel like sharing). Perhaps the robbery might even be connected to a stagecoach robbery that created the phantom stagecoach of Carrizo Wash.

The ghost horse often appears on moonlit nights and seems to be searching for its lost rider.

Buck and Randall are a couple of Texas cowpokes that just like to have fun. Problem is they don't know that they've shuffled off this mortal coil. Even though they're spirits, it hasn't done anything to stop they're prankish ways.

Evidently, if you're camping around the Vallecito Station and you keep finding some of your personal items missing or moved, you can be sure that Buck and Randall are up to their usual tricks. Once a prankster, always a prankster – even in the afterlife. But how did they get that way?

Buck and Randall were Texas cowboys who throughout their travels wound up passing through Vallecito Station on a regular basis and found that they liked the area. Now, from what the local people say, these two were as thick as thieves, compadres to the very end; and one thing they shared was a love of practical jokes, which to the annoyance of the locals, they would pull on a regular basis, each one trying to outdo the other.

This finally got on the nerves of the locals so much that they asked a local distiller to whip up a batch of hooch so potent that when the two cowpokes drank it, the brew might put them out of commission for a while.

They gave this volatile concoction to the two cowboys who were unaware of the ulterior motives behind the gesture. This particular brew was called "Hedgehog Tea" and it tasted sweet, but it had the kick of a mule in alcohol. The locals new better than to even touch the stuff.

That very night, Buck and Randall got more rowdy than normal on the Hedgehog Tea and lost all sense of reason. They whooped and

SECTION

hollered having a good ol' time and this went on most of the night till midnight. They got quiet for a bit, and then, as if having a good belly laugh over some kind of private joke, they both took out their shooting irons, and while still laughing, pointed the guns at each other and shot and killed each other simultaneously. Not the reaction the townsfolk were expecting!

Ever since that night, campers and park rangers have had small objects go missing and one group of campers even had an apparition of a laughing cowboy appear in their tent.

So if your in the area of Vallecito Station, and your flashlight gets misplaced or you can't find your map, just blame it on Buck and Randall and their pranks.

Northeast of Santa Barbara is Santa Ynez, located at the intersection of highways 154 and 246. It's on this narrow road that heads west to Solvang where the sightings of the old stagecoach take place.

In Winchester, Virginia, you'll find the ghostly Shenandoah Stage making its rounds on U.S. Highway 11, heading towards Winchester from New Market.

Carrizo Wash is located off of Highway S2, about sixteen miles north of Ocotillo. Not far away is the Vallecito Station, just four miles northwest of Aqua Caliente, also on Highway S2.

THREE

The Phantom Ford of Netherland Inn Road

As you drive down Netherland Inn Road in Kingsport, Tennessee, on a foggy night, please be careful. Evidently, this stretch of road that runs along the waterfront can be treacherous. Just ask Hugh Hamblen... Oh, that's right; you can't ask Hugh since he died one foggy night on this road back in 1922. But, you might encounter his helpful spirit.

Hugh's sad story both begins and ends on a dark and foggy night in 1922. As most parents, the last thing you want to do is get a phone call from the hospital informing you that your child is injured and in the hospital.

Hugh's son, Charlie had been out drinking and driving around with five of his friends, when the driver of the Ford they were riding in lost control and crashed into the side of a bridge. Four of the other boys died in the crash, but Charlie and another lad were taken to the nearby Kingsport Hospital which was behind the Netherland Inn.

Charlie was severely injured, but Hugh stayed with the boy all night, waiting for some sign of improvement. Finally, towards early morning it was determined that Charlie was out of danger and had every chance of surviving his injuries. Relieved that his son was going to recover, Hugh chose to go back home and get some much-needed rest.

As he walked down the foggy, dark road to his home, Hugh was struck by another vehicle that failed to see him in the fog. Hugh was killed instantly. Charlie, upon hearing of his father's death, felt guilty, and even though he recovered from his accident, he never forgave himself for his father's death. He became a recluse.

Ever since that tragic night, people driving on Netherland Inn Road on dark, foggy nights have come across an overturned antique Ford in the middle of the road, and nearby they are flagged by the sad spirit of Hugh Hamblen, who frantically waves for them to slow down and drive more carefully in hopes that others can avoid his fate.

The Netherland Inn Road runs parallel with the waterfront in Kingsport, Tennessee.

SECTION

Ghost

FOUR

I mentioned at the beginning of the last section that of all the types of travel vocations, sailors and men of the sea seem to be the most historically superstitious. They have their ghost ships, phantom pirates, and tales of cursed seafarers such as the infamous *Flying Dutchman*.

In this section we'll be taking a look at all manner of nautical hauntings. There's truly a large variety of ghostly pirates, haunted cruise liners, and cursed vessels, that will truly "Shiver your timbers!"

Ships

SECTION 2

Ghosts of the Titanic

When you hear the name *Titanic,* most people automatically recognize the massive "unsinkable" ocean liner that was ironically sunk by an iceberg on its maiden transatlantic voyage. But what you may not realize is that in the almost 100 years since that tragic night of April 15, 1912, many people have had paranormal encounters all over the United States, and even the rest of the world, linked to this ship.

The *Titanic* was the most luxurious ship built of its time. It had amenities on board that could rival some of the biggest cruise liners of today. For example, the *Titanic* was fitted with a gymnasium, a grill, a swimming pool, and even a hospital, complete with an operating room. But, for all its luxuries, it lacked one very important item that all cruise ships have now. In fact, it is directly because of the *Titanic* and it's tragic sinking that all cruise ships be equipped with enough lifeboats to accommodate all passengers and crew on-board them.

Here's a cross section of the *Titanic* and an early representation of how it sunk. *Courtesy of Cindy Wolf*

Considered the crown jewel of the White Star Line's fleet of cruise liners, the *Titanic* was a massive 45,328 tons. It was the largest cruise ship in the world in 1912. The *Titanic* was as long as four city blocks and measured 882.5 feet long from bow to aft.

A ship of the *Titanic's* stature could only be helmed by someone with prestige and honor, and that man was Captain E. J. Smith, a veteran Admiral of the White Star Line, who had previously captained the *Olympic*, the sister ship to the *Titanic*. Officials of the White Star Line had managed

FOUR

to convince Admiral Smith to postpone his retirement till after the maiden voyage of the *Titanic* which they greatly wished for him to captain. Smith agreed and on that fateful day of April 10th, 1912, the *Titanic* began her legendary and tragic one-way voyage into history.

The entrance to one of the most haunted *Titanic* Exhibits at the Luxor in Las Vegas. *Courtesy of Cindy Wolf*

Ever since the wreck of the *Titanic* was rediscovered by underwater archaeologists in the 1980s, there have been exhibits all over the world displaying the many personal artifacts, and sometime even parts of the ship that they've been able to salvage from the wreck and restore for public viewing.

When James Cameron's epic film, *Titanic,* was released to theaters, it caused an upswing in public interest in the tragic ship. There were people who were always interested in the fascinating story of the ill-fated ocean liner, but the movie raised interest to a new mass level almost overnight.

To be completely honest, I was not interested in the slightest bit in seeing the movie. Oh, I had heard the story of the *Titanic*, but rather than fascinate me, it actually creeped me out to a point where I had no compulsion to go see it in graphic living color. I can't think of a worse way to die than drowning and I knew from the reviews of the movie that the filmmakers pulled no punches in showing how brutal those 1,500 souls died that fateful night in the sub-zero waters of the north Atlantic.

Due to the number of paranormal incidents surrounding the various *Titanic* exhibits all over the world, it's the general consensus of most paranormal investigators that since the *Titanic* is sitting at the bottom of the Atlantic Ocean, some of the spirits have attached themselves to the personal artifacts and travel with exhibits, haunting whatever location they happen to be visiting.

For example, while the *Titanic* Exhibit was at the Georgia Aquarium for several years, it has had several paranormal incidents associated with it. Even the famed T.A.P.S. *Ghosthunters'* team has done an investigation there a few years ago.

One can't help but wonder why so many people visiting the exhibits in different places have claimed to have eerie feelings while inside the attraction. (Cindy and I visited two of the *Titanic* Exhibits, and of the two, only the one at the Luxor in Las Vegas had any kind of weirdness to it – but, more on that later.)

A spokesperson for the Georgia Aquarium, Meghan Gibbons, believes the *Titanic* exhibit is haunted as do a number of the volunteers who work there. Some of the paranormal things that have convinced them that there are spirits lurking about the exhibit are both from patrons to the exhibit and from staff members. Both groups have felt cold spots in the third-class cabin exhibit. It's where you walk through an area mock-up of what the third -class passengers would have been confined to on board the *Titanic*.

When Cindy and I went through this area of the exhibit at the Luxor in Las Vegas, I personally felt very claustrophobic and felt as though there was a heavy pressure surrounding us. Which is very strange because I'm not one to usually get those feelings. I've gone spelunking and have been underground in a number of different caves and caverns and have never felt as confined as I did in that particular corridor. Cindy also claimed she felt uneasy in that part of the exhibit. Part of it I'm sure is due to the very nature of the tragedy portrayed in there, but it was just too much more than that. The corridor was in no way dark or foreboding, but just walking past the cabin doors, you felt as if someone could walk out of them at any second.

Some people have actually heard footsteps in this area after the exhibit had been closed for the night and volunteers claimed to have seen shadowy figures along this corridor. Security guards have reported hearing the sounds of machinery and engines running similar to those heard on board a working ship. If you've ever been on a large cruise ship,

FOUR

you know that when the ship is running, no matter where you are, there is always some background vibration from the engines, and particularly on the lower decks, you can almost feel the hum of them.

Even more unsettling, a visitor and her cousin were walking through the third-class cabin hallway and they both suddenly felt as though they were rocking back and forth on board a ship. I know that the people who run the *Titanic* Exhibit strive for realism in the mock-ups of parts of the ship, but I think this is a little bit out of their league.

Not only have people felt the exhibit move, but some people claim that as they walk through the halls of the exhibit, they have smelled the fresh tang of seawater in the air. I can vouch for this. I smelled seawater while walking the promenade deck mock-up at the exhibit at the Luxor. At first I thought it was a great touch, but only later did I find out that pumping in the smell of seawater was not part of the exhibit. Cindy was impressed at how realistic the Promenade Deck was recreated, I'm not sure that all of it was due to the builders of the exhibits skill in making it. Some of it just seemed too realistic.

The *Titanic* left on its doomed voyage from the port at Southampton, England.

The Atlantic Paranormal Society, or T.A.P.S. as they are known on the TV show, *Ghosthunters,* did a lengthy investigation of the *Titanic* Exhibit while it was at the Georgia Aquarium. This episode aired on the 97th anniversary of the sinking of the *Titanic*. One of the more interesting finds of the *Ghosthunters'* investigation was an EVP or electronic voice phenomenon that they picked up in one of the exhibit rooms. While trying to communicate with a spirit, Jay and Grant asked if the spirit wanted them to leave. On their digital recorder they clearly heard a voice that said, " Now-please, wait." Unfortunately, they only discovered it later when they were reviewing their evidence at the hotel.

On another occasion, a woman, her daughter, and grandson were visiting the exhibit at the Georgia Aquarium and they had a very disturbing encounter. While viewing the first-class passenger cabin her young grandson kept asking, "Who is that lady in there?" and "What is she doing in there?" They assured him that there was no lady (at least not one they could see), and that there was only a dress laid over the back of the love seat in the cabin to look as though someone were getting ready to go out. It wasn't until the episode of *Ghosthunters* aired on TV did they actually suspect the boy could have been seeing a spirit of a woman in that cabin.

In other *Titanic* Exhibits around the United States and the world many other people have had some close encounters with the spirits of the doomed ship.

A few years ago, a patron visiting the *Titanic* Exhibit in Atlantic City, New Jersey, claimed to have heard a terrified agonizing scream while inside the exhibit and then later, while walking through the room displaying personal artifacts from the person, said they were gripped by a wave of strong emotions and had felt they were experiencing the emotions of people watching the *Titanic* sink from one of the lifeboats.

In New York, New York, when the *Titanic* Exhibit was there, security guards claimed that something or someone invisible to the naked eye kept setting off motion detectors within the halls of the exhibit.

In 2006, at the *Titanic* Museum in Branson, Missouri, a visitor took a picture of his wife standing on the landing of the replicated Grand Ballroom staircase and captured swirls of ectoplasm circling her even though there was nothing visible when he took the picture – oh, and by the way, he took the picture on April 14th the anniversary of the sinking of the *Titanic*.

Even in other countries they have had paranormal experiences with the *Titanic* Exhibit. According to Cheryl Mure, the Exhibition Director of Education, when the exhibit was in Athens, Greece, disembodied English-speaking voices were heard throughout the halls of the exhibit long after they had closed to the public.

In Monterrey, Mexico, many of the volunteers and staff members were puzzled by the claims of at least twenty people who had all praised the authenticity of a man dressed as a officer of the *Titanic* who answered their questions as if he'd been aboard the ship. The problem was the staff didn't know of any re-enactors in the exhibit at that time and when they went to look for him, there was no trace that he'd ever been there.

FOUR

The other exhibit Cindy and I have been to was the one in Bermuda at the Bermuda Underwater Institute in Hamilton. While the one in Bermuda was very interesting and was my first exposure to some of the artifacts from the *Titanic,* I can't really say that I or Cindy felt there was anything paranormal surrounding the exhibit. If there was were, we certainly had no encounters with it. On the other hand, going through the exhibit at the Luxor in Las Vegas was a totally different experience.

I purposely chose not to do any research on hauntings of the *Titanic* Exhibits until I had gone through the one in Vegas because I didn't want to have any preconceived notions of what to look for in paranormal activity.

Cindy was actually surprised that I wanted to go through the exhibit because all the previous times we were out in Vegas I was opposed to going through it. I have to be totally honest, as much as I'm into ghost hunting and have no problem with going into a haunted location or graveyard at night, I had really been apprehensive about going to this exhibit. Ever since I was a child I've had this eerie feeling about drowning and for some reason, and to this day I can't explain why, no other shipwreck or ship gives me the uneasy feeling that the *Titanic* does. But, by the same token I'm also fascinated by the *Titanic*.

My first impression of the exhibit was that they really spared no expense in recreating the areas of the ship. I could easily see why people would become disoriented in this place. Once you pass the recreation of the dock at Southampton, you immediately are inside a corridor that mimics the third-class passenger area of the ship. This cramped, but well lit, corridor has a distinct oppressive feel to it. If you've ever been on the lower decks of a cruise ship you'll realize the builders of the exhibit did a top-notch job of recreating this. I thought they had the feel of being inside the ship perfect, but if some of the accounts of other visitors are to be believed, then there may be more than meets the eye to this mock-up. I remember commenting to Cindy as to how much it felt like being on a ship this area felt, I even felt as if the ship was moving and she agreed how authentic it looked and felt.

As we walked through the twisting halls of the exhibit looking at various pieces of memorabilia from the doomed ship, as well as articles about the ship itself, we couldn't help but wonder who some of these poor souls might have been.

One of the most impressive rooms in the exhibit is the recreation of the Grand Ballroom staircase. It's so popular that everyone wants to have their picture taken while standing on it. There is a staff person on hand to take your picture should you want one, considering they don't allow you to take any pictures with your own camera inside the exhibition.

According to some of the volunteers and staff members of the exhibit, there's a mysterious apparition of a woman dressed in black period clothing of the early twentieth century who has been sighted. Apparently, she has some unfinished business with the "Unsinkable" Molly Brown. The woman in black cries out for Molly Brown from the first-class gallery.

There's a fascinating room where they have a scale model of the *Titanic* as it sits on the bottom of the ocean. You get the feel that you are looking at the ship from an undersea vessel. In this same room, there are more artifacts salvaged from the wreck, including a display of dishes that miraculously were not only unbroken, but it seems that as they settled on the bottom of the sea they actually stayed stacked in close order! The apparition of a teenaged boy has been seen in this area of the exhibit although no-one has a clue as to who he might have been on board the ship.

In the Iceberg room, not surprisingly there is a large chunk of ice with hand prints embedded in the side of it (very creepy!). A volunteer named Maureen Mourino was sitting near the exhibit when she felt something stir and move behind her. Then she felt as though someone had put their hands on the top of her scalp. In her words, "It was like a swimming cap was on my head." Considering it was after the exhibit had closed for the night and there was no one else around, she feels it was definitely some kind of paranormal encounter with one of the lost souls from aboard the Titanic.

If you visit the *Titanic* Exhibit and feel as though some one has put their hand on your shoulder when nobody else is around, don't feel frightened – it's just the sad spirit of Frederick Fleet making sure you're okay.

Supposedly, the ghost of Frederick Fleet haunts the *Titanic* Exhibit at the Luxor, even though he never died on the *Titanic*. Frederick Fleet was one of the lookouts on the *Titanic* who missed spotting the enormous iceberg which caused the unsinkable ocean liner to sink. Far too late to make any difference he shouted, "Iceberg! Right ahead!"

Much to his guilty conscience he was one of the few survivors of that tragic night and had spent the rest of his natural life wrongly feeling guilty for the ship sinking. At the age of 78, Fleet's conscience could no

FOUR

longer handle the years of self-inflicted guilt and he committed suicide after many years of undeserved grief.

Since then, Frederick Fleet's spirit has been thought to be one of the many ghosts who haunt the *Titanic* exhibit at the Luxor. He's been known to touch everybody who comes to visit the exhibit, making sure they're okay before they leave. Perhaps this makes his afterlife a little more bearable.

Should you feel the need to get even closer to the poor souls who died on the *Titanic*, you'll have to wait a little longer. There is a memorial cruise from Fred Olsen Cruises that will be visiting the site that the *Titanic* went down in 1912. In April 2012, one hundred years after the original White Star Liner hit an iceberg and sunk. Unfortunately, as soon as ticket sales were announced the cruise sold out. Some of the people on board will be actual descendants of some of the passengers who perished that night.

On the very spot where the *Titanic* went down, they also plan to have a memorial service at the exact time the ship struck the iceberg. Even more unsettling (to me, anyway.) is the fact that the parent company of the cruise line offering the tour is Harland & Wolff, the same company who built the *Titanic*!

> There are many different *Titanic* Exhibits throughout the world. Some other places that have shown or are showing *Titanic* Exhibits are: Orlando, Florida; Branson, Missouri; London, England; Tucson, Arizona, and several other places.

SECTION

The Queen Mary

If the *Titanic* is the Granddaddy of ghost ships then *The Queen Mary* is the Grandmother. Granted, *The Queen Mary* is now a dry-docked floating hotel, but in her many years of dedicated service, she's seen tragedy and triumph and has more than a few skeletons and ghosts in her closets.

The Queen Mary was commissioned for service in 1936 as an ocean liner. It started out as transatlantic cruise ship similar to the *Titanic*. But during WWII, it served a totally different purpose: It was painted a drab shade of gray and was used as a troop transport.

The RMS *Queen Mary* made an unprecedented 1,001 transatlantic crossings in thirty one years of service until it was finally dry docked as a floating hotel in Long Beach, California. *The Queen Mary's* days as an ocean-going vessel may be long past, but the numerous hauntings and unexplained paranormal events show that it is still on active duty in the afterlife.

According to psychic Peter James, there are over 600 lost souls that are actively haunting *The Queen Mary.* With so many spirits, it's hard to talk about all of them or to even know who all of them are. So what I'd like to do is focus on some of the most well known spirits and where they are most likely to be found aboard the ship.

While there are a few decidedly more haunted places than others aboard the ship, all over the ship at any time of the day or night you might have a run-in with one of the spirits. Many people have said that just walking along the passageways of the ship they've felt cold spots, smelled cigar smoke, even though there is a strict non-smoking policy on the entire ship, and have heard disembodied voices when no one else was around. Visitors and staff alike have also heard strange pounding noises coming from the hull of the ship. Many guests staying aboard the floating hotel have found personal items that have mysteriously moved from one place to another. Not to be left out, some staff members in the administration offices have claimed to have papers strewn about the room after everyone has left

FOUR

for the night. Both guests and hotel staff have seen full and partial apparitions throughout the ship, but there are some popular locations such as the kitchen, first-class swimming pool, and the engine room, where some of the more active spirits make themselves known.

In the first-class lounge, there are several different spirits in residence. First, there's a spirit of a beautiful, young woman who has a habit of wearing a long, flowing white dress as she floats across the room. Many people have also spotted what looks to be a very dapper, black-haired man wearing formal clothes that look like they're from the 1930s. Even if these spirits aren't seen, many people have seen bright orbs of light floating in this area of the ship.

One of the most haunted areas of the ship is the first-class pool area. Several spirits call this section of the ship home. A pair of female ghosts have been sighted lounging about the pool. It's presumed that both of them died from drowning. The one ghost, Jackie, is a young girl who was thought to have drowned in the second-class pool, but has repeatedly been spotted in the first-class pool area with an older woman named Sarah.

Jackie's spirit originated in the 1930s and she is usually dressed in clothing from that time period. Jackie is a very active spirit and has even interacted with some of the guests touring the ship on one of the regularly scheduled haunted tours of the ship. On one of the tours, a female tourist bought a gift of a toy doll for the little girl's spirit to play with. The doll had a bright ribbon tied around its neck and the tourist proceeded to video tape the doll. During this video, the ribbon was pulled off the doll by the unseen ghostly hands of Jackie, who must have been thrilled to have gotten a toy to play with over the last seventy years as a spirit. According to Peter James, who was conducting the tour, he has a copy of this amazing video.

Not to be ignored, though, is the spirit of Sarah, a middle-aged female spirit that also haunts the first-class pool area. She is dressed in clothing from the sixties, so her drowning in the pool must have occurred during the latter days of the cruise liner's final days as a sea-going vessel, since *The Queen Mary* was dry docked in 1967. She was perturbed by the fact that most people seem to think that Jackie was the only spirit in the vicinity of the pool. One time, claims Peter James, he was trying to contact the spirit of Jackie when he was slapped on the arm so hard it left a welt. That's when he was introduced to the not so happy spirit of Sarah. Evidently, Sarah is very territorial and feels that this particular section of the ship is hers and is very angry that people invade her privacy.

Another psychic hot spot (so to speak), is cabin B340. This guest cabin has proven to be so paranormally active that the owners of *The Queen Mary* no longer rent it out. Supposedly, this room is haunted by the spirit of a Purser who had been murdered in the cabin. But on the episode of *Ghosthunters*, the T.A.P.S team were told that it was a guest who was found dead in the cabin in 1948 that haunts the room. Regardless of how it became haunted, people who have stayed in the room always complained of being uncomfortable and of being aware of someone watching them in the night. They even have said that while they were sleeping, something would tear the covers off the bed and throw them on the floor in the middle of the night. After the room no longer was in use as guest quarters, the cleaning staff reported that even when they made up the bed, someone or something kept messing it up.

The kitchen is another paranormally active location. While most people who go through this area don't normally see anything paranormal, many people have heard strange screams that date back to an incident that happened during WWII, when *The Queen Mary* was a troop transport.

The military assigned a crewman as a cook, who would have probably been better off swabbing the decks, because his cooking was so bad that even dirty mop water probably would've tasted better by a long shot. This cook's chow was so horrible that after their requests for a new cook, the crew who had to eat his food became a ravenous, unruly mob that stormed the kitchen, took the cook captive and then as things sometimes do when mob rules get out of hand, they stuffed him in his own oven, turned on the gas and burnt him to death.

People touring the kitchen have said that they can still hear the poor (in more ways than one), cook's agonizing screams as they happened almost sixty long years ago.

Even the ship's morgue has had supernatural encounters. Over the years, people have claimed to hear disembodied voices and have been touched and pushed or shoved while in this area of *The Queen Mary*.

FOUR

One place that is haunted that can be pointed to in particular is in the engineering section of the ship – its Hatchway Door #13. In 1966, the ship was having a routine safety drill which included automatically sealing some of the hatches in case of hull breaches to keep the ship from flooding.

During one of these drills, a young man named John Pedder was caught in between one of these hatches as it closed upon him, and with crushing force trapped him, killing him instantly. It's his sad spirit that people have encountered in this hatchway.

Then there's the spirit of Second Officer William Stark, who died a painful self-inflicted poisoning death when he inadvertently drank some tetrachloride that had been stored in an old bottle of Gin.

All over *The Queen Mary,* throughout the years, many people have had some sort of paranormal encounters, whether with some of the more well-known spirits or just the random sight of body parts. Rest assured that should you decide to visit or stay at this huge monument to ocean travel, you will more than likely have some sort of run in with a spirit or two.

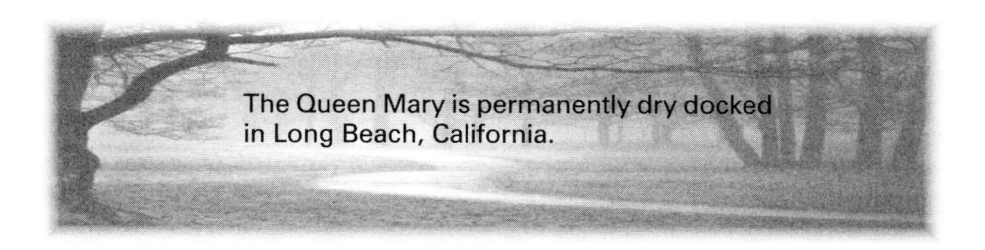

The Queen Mary is permanently dry docked in Long Beach, California.

SECTION

Haunted

FIVE

Another top pick of haunted places are bridges. Why so many bridges are considered prime haunting grounds for spirits is up to debate. Perhaps it's the amount of people who choose to end their lives by jumping off a bridge. Then again, a large number of accidents tend to happen on bridges and the victims of these accidents might still be confused and lingering on the bridge in the afterlife. Be it a large bridge like the Brooklyn Bridge or just a small local covered bridge like Sach's Mill Bridge in Gettysburg, spirits seem to have an affinity to manifesting themselves in these places. Maybe they just like the sound of running water.

Bridges

Sachs Mill Bridge in Gettysburg

Sachs Mill Bridge may not be as famous as some other locations in Gettysburg, such as Devil's Den, Cemetery Ridge, or even Little Round Top, but what it lacks in historical notoriety, it more than makes up for as a paranormal hot spot. In an area known for hauntings, Sachs Mill Bridge holds its own mysteries of the paranormal.

Sachs Mill Bridge was built in 1854 or 1852 (reports vary), by a man named David Stoner. The bridge itself is in the design of a covered bridge found in many places in the United States and in a great quantity in the Pennsylvania Dutch areas of the east coast. It's 100 feet long and spans over Marsh Creek. Initially, it was built to help the local farmers transport their crops over the creek. But during the battle of Gettysburg, it had a far more gruesome utility and this is where most of the stories of it being haunted originate. I say most because even before the Civil War the Marsh Creek had a tragic ghost story attached to it: one that involves a particularly tragic buggy accident.

Not too far from Sachs Mill Bridge, there is another bridge that crosses Marsh Creek on the Fairfield Road. Long before the Battle of Gettysburg, a young, pretty woman by the name of Peggy Noel was riding her horse and buggy home very late at night. No one is sure of why she was out at such a late hour of the night. It's been speculated by some that she was visiting a prospective beau or perhaps she was coming from a late night dance in the town of Gettysburg (although in that time period, it was unusual for a woman to be out by herself late at night unescorted). So perhaps she was helping care for a sick neighbor, or as some with a more scandalous view thought, she might have been having a secret affair.

We'll never know what she was doing out there that night, but what we do know is that on her journey she lost control of the horses pulling the buggy and through some tragic twist of fate, as the buggy ran off the road and plunged into Marsh Creek, poor Ms. Noel literally lost her head in the accident. She must have died instantly. So unexpectantly was her demise that her spirit never left the bridge where the accident occurred.

FIVE

Over many, many years, fishermen and others who have been in or near Marsh Creek have described seeing the headless specter of poor Peggy Noel splashing around in the waters of the creek. Usually, her cranium-deprived ghost is spotted in the springtime and more than one early morning fisherman has encountered her over the years, just not face-to-face.

During the battle of Gettysburg, Sachs Mill Bridge was used by both the Union and the Confederacy. Abner Doubleday's Division for the Union used the bridge to get to the battlefield and Longstreet used it to get troops to the battle or the Confederacy. After the 2nd day of fighting, the bridge remained behind the Confederate lines and when they were forced to retreat, they used the bridge and the area around it as a hospital for the wounded.

My first trip to Sachs Mill Bridge was in March of 1998. I had been to Gettysburg many times but I had never heard of this location. It was on an investigation with Pennsylvania Ghost Hunters Society that I was introduced to this haunted site. It was also where I first used a EMF detector.

Our group consisted of Rick Fisher, the President of the PGHS, myself, and a dozen or so other members of our group. We were there scouting locations for investigating during the 1st Gettysburg Ghost Conference that the PGHS was hosting that year.

I had just bought my first EMF detector and was looking forward to using it at Sachs Mill Bridge. Until this point, I had always had to borrow other people's ghost hunting gear and now I had some of my very own. Granted this was a very simple version of an electromagnetic field detector. It worked with only three indicator lights: Green meant no EMF, yellow meant low level EMF, and red meant high level of EMF. What I was told by Rick and some of the other more experienced members of our group was that the yellow light is what I wanted to see. That would indicate that there was a possible spirit near the detector. That is if I wasn't in close proximity to something that would give of an EMF field naturally, like exposed wires or other appliances that used electricity. But out there, in the middle of nowhere, there was no chance I'd run into any of that sort of interference, they informed me.

Once we arrived, the eeriness of the site was palpable. The covered bridge was surrounded by a dense fog as we approached. You could hear the water gurgling underneath it's trusses, but you couldn't see it.

SECTION

Every so often, a break in the fog would allow the full moon to shine on the structure bathing it in a luminous silver glow.

We received a quick briefing from Rick about the do's and don'ts of ghost hunting and then we fanned out across and onto the bridge to do our various equipment readings and to get a general feel for the location. I took off on my own and headed through the dense fog to the far side of the bridge, opposite from where the cars were parked. Some people chose to work together combining equipment such as digital cameras and recorders or digital scanning thermometers and cameras. I wanted to work alone, away from everyone else, for a little while just to see how my EMF meter worked by itself.

I'll admit that I felt a small chill in the air as I walked blindly into the fog. I was so intent on watching the lights on my EMF detector that I really wasn't paying attention to where I was going. I don't recommend doing that but, as I said it was one of the first times I had used the EMF meter and was not using common sense. Usually, it's not a good idea to wander off by yourself during an investigation, but I chose to ignore that rule as well. You've got to understand that ghost hunting groups were still new back then and we didn't have the hindsight we do nowadays. There were no shows like *Ghosthunters* or *Ghost Adventures* on TV back then.

So there I was, wandering around near Marsh Creek in a dense fog at night. Like I said, in retrospect, not the brightest activity in the world to be doing. But, then I struck gold! As I walked towards a particular tree I noticed that the yellow LED light on my EMF detector lit up. As far as I knew there would have been no normal reason for it to do that. I started looking around for possible sources such as electric wires or telephone poles, but there were none to be found. So I tried an experiment. I walked towards the same tree as I had gotten a reading from and kept walking until the light changed color. I was right at the base of the tree which was on the creek bank and I was still getting a yellow reading. As I moved away from the tree the light changed back to green, which meant there was no EMF in the area. I turned around and started walking towards the tree again, and sure enough, as I reached the base of the tree, the light changed from green to yellow again! Just to be sure I repeated the experiment one more time with the same results. Incredible!

The fog was starting to burn off, so I returned to where the other members of PGHS were gathered on the bridge. Evidently I wasn't the only one to have success in capturing the paranormal at the bridge that night. Rick Fisher had captured several orbs and some ectoplasm on

FIVE

his digital camera. Some other people had captured some very good EVPs and one person, named Andy, had actually heard a disembodied voice crying for help. When I told them about my experience with the EMF detector and the tree, Tom, another member of PGHS told me that supposedly, Confederate deserters were captured and executed by hanging them from one of the trees near this very bridge after the battle of Gettysburg. At the very least I discovered that the area around Sachs Mill Bridge was used as a makeshift field hospital.

We eventually left the site later that night, but considering all the paranormal evidence we'd collected, we felt that it was a good location to take groups of people from the Ghost Conference to, and sure enough, people from the conference had quite a few paranormal encounters there. We even had some people claim that they had gotten some very good responses from using pendulums and other occult devices such as Ouija boards.

This was taken during an investigation of Sachs's Mill bridge by the Pennsylvania Ghost Hunters Society. Notice the kite-like ectoplasm in the upper right of the picture.

We weren't the only ones to have paranormal encounters at Sachs Mill Bridge. According to Elizabeth Matusiak in her book: *The Battlefield Dead*, some tourists who had never been to Gettysburg before had a chilling encounter at Sach's Mill Bridge one night.

While visiting the bridge at night the two men had a paranormal encounter that started off with an unexplainable eerie fog creeping across the field near the bridge. Unexplainable because there was no fog anywhere else in the vicinity of the bridge, or creek for that matter. This "fog" seemed to have a definite purpose; it was heading directly towards them!

What happened next was even more amazing and frightening. Out of this ball of fog stepped three Confederate soldiers. According to the eye witnesses, (which by the way had no interest in the paranormal before that night), it looked as though one of these soldiers was severely wounded and was being helped along by the other two soldiers on either side of him. The tourists described them as shabbily dressed and looking weary.

As the shocked men watched this eerie procession from another time, the wounded Confederate soldier looked at them with pleading eyes and they both heard him clearly say, "Help us." That was all it took to totally unnerve the two modern-day observers. They only remember running away at that point and couldn't even tell where they were running to. Just that they had to get out of there and fast, lest they get caught up in that ethereal moment forever.

Perhaps it was the spirits of these unfortunate Confederate soldiers that my fellow PGHS member, Andy, heard on the night we had been there scouting the bridge as a site for the Ghost Conference.

Many people who have visited this bridge have heard whispers, disembodied footsteps, and have even seen dark shadow-like figures over the years.

So if you ever take the small side trip from the more famous sites of the Gettysburg Battlefield and come across and old covered bridge, listen closely and you may hear a faint cry for help echoing over the decades since the battle took place there.

Sachs Mill Bridge is in Gettysburg, Pennsylvania. It spans Marsh Creek at Waterworks Road. It is a short distance from the main battlefield, but well worth the trip.

FIVE

The Temptress of Old Birdsboro Bridge

Near Baumstown in Berks County, Pennsylvania, there used to be an old wooden bridge where a veiled female spirit enticed people to their doom. The bridge is gone, but the approach to the bridge is still there and if you continue driving along the road you'll fall to your death. Which is exactly what this spirit wants to happen so she can have some companionship in the afterlife, or so the story has been told for over a hundred years.

The old Birdsboro Bridge is long gone, but that hasn't stopped the spirit of a young woman from making her appearance. *Courtesy of Cindy Wolf*

According to some eye witnesses, the female spirit is actually very vocal. Before the old wooden bridge was destroyed, her spirit used to stop horse and buggies that were trying to cross the bridge over the Schuylkill River.

To be precise, the bridge is actually near the center of Birdsboro. Birdsboro was founded by Iron master William Bird in 1737. After William Bird died, his son, Marcus, took over the family business of forging and started the now-historic Hopewell Forge to the south of Birdsboro.

Even though Birdsboro is a quaint, small town, there have been some very famous people who came from here. One of the most famous was Daniel Boone. The Daniel Boone homestead is a very historic site and is haunted in its own right, but that would be beyond the scope of this book since none of the spirits haunt anyplace outside of the homestead.

The woman's spirit has been seen for over 100 years, so whatever caused her spirit to linger in this location had its start early in the eighteenth century. By most accounts, she always wears a veil over her face and has a habit of walking right up to a vehicle. So she isn't shy.

We know of her practice of talking to strangers, but where did this spirit come from? Though the original bridge is gone, we'll have to presume that she is somehow attached to that bridge, rather than the new modern one that spans over the Schuylkill River. Did she perhaps have some sort of accident on that original bridge? She seems like the sociable type of spirit, so she's not a mindless ghost, just reenacting her death.

To get to the bottom of this mysterious spirit, I decided to visit the old Birdsboro Bridge in person, and believe me it wasn't very easy to find. I set out on a chilly, but sunny, day in November thinking: How hard can it be to find this bridge? After all. There's a town by the same name so the bridge can't be too far from it. How wrong I was.

After winding through a long tree-lined country road called Route 345. I eventually arrived at the small borough of Birdsboro. That's not too hard to find as the road I was on became a T intersection and to the right there was open ground and to the left there were buildings. I turned left and headed into the small town passing a few residential homes that looked like they were built at least a hundred years ago, if not longer. To be sure, there were some modern buildings including a Mexican restaurant.

My problem was I couldn't find my way to this old Birdsboro Bridge that my research was talking about. Granted, like a typical guy, I don't usually stop and ask for directions, but I still wanted to see if I could find this bridge on my own before giving in. I did cross over a modern paved bridge, but according to my research, both on the Internet and in some of my ghost lore books, the road I should be looking for was South Baumstown Road. I found this road shortly after crossing the bridge and drove down it hoping to find some sort of indication as to where this enigmatic old bridge would be.

Finally, I came to the end of the road (literally, the road ended and intersected with Route 422). I turned around in someone's driveway and headed back the way I came only to come back to the same bridge where I started. I thought that maybe I would see something coming the

FIVE

opposite way, but no such luck. This bridge was becoming almost as difficult to find as a ghost itself.

I wasn't thinking or I would've tried to find the local library. Instead I headed back down the road to the south and after a few miles stopped in at the Hopewell Furnace State Historical Site. Thinking I might find some local history pamphlet or book, I browsed through the gift shop/museum, while a park ranger talked to an older couple of tourists. I figured if I couldn't find a book, perhaps the park ranger was a local and could fill me in as to where this bridge was. Turns out he was an excellent source of information.

According to the park ranger, the reason I was having a problem finding the correct bridge is that the road designations had changed and that what was once Route 82 was changed to Route 724/345 and went right past South Baumstown Road where the old Route 82 once did. He further went on to explain that there had been another older bridge there that was wiped out in 1926 under mysterious circumstances. Even though this would've been long after the ghost sightings had already been recorded, perhaps this might have something to do with the female spirit after all.

A few days later, I decided to make another attempt at finding this elusive old bridge approach and this time I had an ace up my sleeve. This time I was bringing Cindy with me. I figured between the two of us we'd be able to find this place. I followed the directions the Park Ranger gave me, and after a half hour's drive through the country road leading to Main Street in Birdsboro, we arrived at the spot the Park Ranger directed me to. I knew there was no place to park on the new bridge so I parked the car at a nearby Turkey Hill convenience store, and making sure I locked the car, I had Cindy grab our digital camera and we set off to find the Temptress of the Old Birdsboro Bridge.

It was only a short hike from the parking lot at the Turkey Hill to the bridge. Now you have to realize that this isn't the bridge I was looking for. This was a newer version of the Old Birdsboro Bridge and I was hoping to find some remnant of the old bridge. Even so, this bridge wasn't that all that new. A friend of mine, Keith Smoker, lives in Birdsboro and I tried to pick his brain for any stories connected with the old bridge. He did his best to come up with some leads for me, but sadly he didn't know anyone who had encounters with the female spirit that haunts the old bridge. He would've been happy to meet us at the bridge, but he had to work the day we had scheduled to explore it and I was on a tight schedule.

SECTION 7

This is a small side bridge off of the main Birdsboro Bridge. Perhaps the woman's spirit uses this less traffic laden bridge to lure people in.

    The new Birdsboro Bridge spans over the Schuylkill River and there's a small island to the one side of the bridge with a small and very old bridge extension that leads to it. This is where I wanted to go. I thought maybe if I could get to that old island, I might be able to see where the old bridge used to be. Thankfully, we didn't have to dodge any traffic walking the bridge as there is a sidewalk for pedestrians who need to use the bridge.

    Cindy felt that it was best to check on both sides of the bridge to see if we could spot the remnants of the old bridge. One side looked promising. There was actually another older bridge further on down the river, but I knew that this wasn't the bridge we were looking for. For one thing, the bridge was still there and I was looking for just a partial bridge.

    We finally made it down to the island. As we walked down the old decrepit and crumbling bridge extension, Cindy thought that we could've probably brought our car down, but I thought otherwise. This section just looked too unstable. Parts of the sides were severely crumbling off. It looked to me like something you'd see in one of those nuclear apocalypse movies. I half expected to be attacked by some crazed radiated, zombies. This kind of thinking wasn't doing me any good and I wasn't going to mention it to Cindy because she was already voicing her concern about "Bad People" hiding out down here and I did have to admit it was pretty isolated, even for being right off a major road. This did look like the perfect spot for some crazed serial killer to hide a body or two...brr!

FIVE

Although you can drive down the old bridge, it is very narrow and I certainly wouldn't recommend doing it. Especially if you want to make a quick retreat from the female spirit that resides there. *Courtesy of Cindy Wolf*

I did want to get a look around though and even though the area was overgrown I thought I might spot some clue as to where this old bridge could be. We both scanned the area, but I'll admit we really didn't come up with any concrete evidence for the old bridge. In the end, we took a bunch of pictures and hoped that maybe something would show up on them that could give us a clue.

Going down there at night alone is not something I would recommend doing. There's too many places that dangerous people could ambush you from. Even going in a group is probably not advisable, but if you do feel the need to go there at night in a group and you end up having a paranormal encounter with the spirit that haunts the bridge, please feel free to contact me and tell me of your encounter.

The Birdsboro Bridge is located in Birdsboro, Berks County. The bridge is a concrete arch bridge over the Schuylkill River on State Road 345. The bridge is slated for demolition and to be rebuilt.

SECTION

Cry-Baby Bridges

If hitchhiking ghosts are the most popular urban legends across the country, then cry-baby bridges have got to be a very close second. In all my research for this book, I have come across more references to this type of haunting than any other. I don't know what the fascination is with babies haunting bridges, but seriously, because of the sheer amount of infant deaths occurring on bridges, there should be a federal law banning babies from crossing bridges.

So here's the general scoop. Most of these cry-baby bridges share a similar story. Typically, the mother of the baby either purposefully or accidentally drops her newborn infant over a bridge into a lake or river where the child drowns. After that fate, the baby's spirit is trapped on the bridge and either pushes cars, makes a crying sound, and if you leave candy for this ghost child, it will take it and leave the candy wrapper behind as proof.

Alabama's Stories

Alabama has several of these cry-baby bridges for example: In Clanton there's a legend about a dark, foggy night during the Civil War when a woman was being chased by some men who wanted to kill her baby. Why they wanted to do this, we don't know. But, in order to keep the men from killing her baby, she tossed it in a little creek and the baby died. (Does this even make sense?) Ever since then, if you go on to the bridge at night and leave an unwrapped candy bar sitting on there and then turn your back, wait a few minutes, and look back... Surprise! Your candy bar will be gone. Amazing! Some people also claim to hear a baby crying and others say you can see the shadow of a baby in the water. I'm not sure how you could see the shadow at night. I have a hard enough time seeing things in the water in the daytime, let alone trying to spot some shadow in the water after dark.

FIVE

A variation to this story is attached to Cullman, Alabama's Cry Baby Hollow. The story harks back to the early pioneer days when Cullman was being settled. A hearty family of homesteaders were trying to cross a small wooden bridge when a wheel broke and the wagon overturned, tossing the family's newborn baby into the creek and it died instantly. Now, if you go to this bridge and put down a candy bar, a bite will be taken out of it. You can also hear the sound of a baby crying. (Perhaps, it really just a strange sounding animal.)

Just in Alabama, I know of six cry-baby bridges/hollows/creeks, and the list goes on and on in other states. Arkansas has at least two cry-baby bridges. From what I can gather, almost every state in the United States has some form of cry-baby bridge. Sometimes there is also has a female spirit that coexists alongside the ghost baby, but many times the ghost of the infant is by itself. There's even a few cry-baby bridges that cross over into the realm of being a gravity hill, because the ghost infant will sometimes push a car parked in neutral across the bridge and will leave tiny, infant-sized hand prints on the bumper of the car. Talk about a supernatural baby!

I'm sure that most of these accounts of cry-baby bridges are just local legends. But, there's nothing wrong with having a good urban legend spice up some otherwise dull history.

Ghostly

SIX

If there's a who's who of the spirit world then ghostly hitchhikers would have a definite listing as the most popular type of haunting. All over the USA and around the world from ancient times, hitchhiking spirits have made their presence known to unwary travelers. Some of the most famous ghost stories in history have been about hitchhiking ghosts. Resurrection Mary in Chicago might well be one of the most famous spirits in history, but there are quite a few other ghostly hitchhikers out there and not all of them are as pleasant as Mary.

Hitchhikers

SECTION

Midnight Mary of Bordentown Road

One of the strangest tales of ghostly hitchhikers is the tale of Midnight Mary. It takes place along a stretch of road in Pennsylvania near the New Jersey border called Bordentown Road. Now, don't get me wrong; Midnight Mary has been spotted along this road, but she also has a penchant for dancing...on Van Sciver Lake!

It's along this stretch of Bordentown Road that motorists have encountered Midnight Mary.

Here's one version of the story: Back in the mid 1930s, a young woman was killed in a horrific car accident while coming back from a prom. The story goes that she and her date were driving down Bordentown Road when whoever was driving (some people say she was; others say it was her date) lost control of the vehicle and crashed it into the lake. While they found the boy's body, the girl's body was never recovered.

Ever since that tragic night, her spirit has been seen either floating or gliding along Bordentown Road hitchhiking in a sopping-wet pink prom dress.

Now, to coin a Paul Harvey tag line...Here's the rest of the story: One of the biggest revelations is that Mary is probably not her real name. There's no record of any accident victims of the late 1930s named Mary

SIX

in the area, but there *is* one listed for a young woman named Gertrude Louise Spring. Ms. Spring and her boyfriend were killed in a car accident on Bordentown Road in 1935. The only thing is, there are a few different details concerning the accident.

The basics of the incident remains the same. Gertrude Spring and her boyfriend, named by some people as William Bagley, were killed in a car accident on Bordentown Road, near Van Sciver Lake. But where fact takes over from fiction, there's some serious discrepancies in the story.

Seeing how Gertrude was twenty-six years old at the time of the accident, it's a pretty good guess that she wasn't returning home from her prom as the legend suggests. According to a newspaper article written at the time of the accident, Ms. Spring might have actually been the driver of the vehicle and they were coming back from dinner at another couple's home. They had attended the Devon Horse Show earlier that day. So it is possible that Gertrude was formally dressed in a pink gown as a lot of the eyewitnesses to the haunting say she is, and not a prom dress.

Sometimes Midnight Mary likes to dance on the water of Van Sciver Lake.

For one thing, the unfortunate couple didn't drive into the lake as the urban legend would have you believe. They actually crashed into a tree along the side of the road and Mr. Bagley was thrown from the vehicle on impact and died instantly on the scene. Gertrude, however, was a bit more lucky – at least in some respect. She had also suffered some heavy injuries, but at least the ambulance crew was able to get her out of the mangled car and drive her to the nearby hospital in Trenton, New Jersey.

Gertrude lingered for days before she died on May 31st from her injuries sustained in the accident. So there's no truth to the legend that her body was never found. Her mortal remains are buried in St. James Episcopal Church at the corner of Walnut and Cedar Streets.

Many people over the years, although they've never actually seen "Midnight Mary," have had some strange encounters on Bordentown Road along the lake. They've had weird feelings and have seen orbs floating down the road. They've also seen strange flashes of light that seemed to appear out of nowhere and have heard odd sounds.

Ten years after the accident is when the first authentic sighting of Midnight Mary was reported. A motorist driving late one night on Bordentown Road, near Van Sciver Lake, claimed to have seen a young woman, dressed in a pink gown walking aimlessly alongside the road. Since it was late at night and the road was fairly isolated, he thought the nice thing to do would be to stop and offer her a ride. As he took his eyes off of her for only a second to find a place to pull over and offer her a ride, he looked back and she was nowhere to be seen; she had just vanished into thin air. Not surprisingly, he was disturbed by this and looked around thinking that she might have fallen or something worse, but there was no sign of the woman. Eventually, he started feeling strange and just decided to get out of there and took off in his car, shaking his head in wonder at what had just happened.

Not long after that incident, a trucker was doing a late night run down the same road and saw a woman walking alongside the road dressed in a pink gown and looking very much out of place in such a remote area, especially at that time of night.

He stopped the truck and offered the young woman a ride. She gratefully accepted the ride, although she didn't say much, beyond that she wanted to be taken to a house on Radcliffe Avenue in town.

After a short drive, they arrived at the destination, but as a surprise to the driver, she refused to get out of the cab of the truck. Finally, he knocked on the door at the address she requested to be taken to and an old man, disheveled and sleepy, answered the door cautiously. The trucker explained that a woman claiming to be the old man's daughter was refusing to get out of the cab of his truck. This shocked the old man to full wakefulness as he heard this and proceeded to explain to this stranger that his daughter couldn't possibly be in his truck, because she had died ten years earlier. The old man's name? It was Louis Spring, the father of Gertrude Spring. Not convinced of what he was hearing, the trucker insisted they go back

SIX

to the truck and he'd prove to the old man that there really was a young woman in his truck. They both got a shock! The cab was empty, but it looked as though someone had just recently left the vehicle.

Just recently, on one of the many paranormal websites on the Internet, an anonymous poster claims to have lived in a big farmhouse on Bordentown Road near Van Sciver Lake and had this story to tell.

Years ago when she was very young, she and her four sisters lived in a big farmhouse, and once, in the middle of the night, the family was awakened to the sound of someone trying to break into the home via one of the upstairs windows. The girl and all of her sisters ran downstairs in a panic and tried to call the police. The oldest sister claimed that while she was dialing the phone which was right next to a large window, she looked out and spotted a woman dressed in a sopping-wet gown and splattered with mud. The woman looked directly at the girl on the phone and said, "Go ahead, call the police. It's not going to do any good!" Then abruptly vanished. The police arrived shortly, and after conducting an extensive search, never found a sign of any intruder.

I wanted to see for myself if there was any truth to the legend of Midnight Mary, so Cindy and I took a day trip to Bristol, Pennsylvania, to see what facts we could uncover. The trip from our house in East Earl to Bristol was fairly easy. We decided to go on a Sunday so that we wouldn't run into as much turnpike traffic going towards Philadelphia.

We couldn't have asked for better weather. Sometimes the fall can be cold and rainy. But today it was in the low seventies and sunny. After an hour or so, we finally arrived in Bristol and to tell you the truth, I had no clue as to where we had to go. I was relying on our GPS unit in the car and an old Pennsylvania road atlas that was probably older than I was. Cindy was as lost as I was. She had never been to this part of the state, either. Just goes to show, we've traveled all over the U.S. and the U.K. But that doesn't mean we still can't get lost in our own backyard.

Between looking at my old road atlas and the GPS, we did find Bordentown Road where Midnight Mary is supposed to make her appearance. I'll admit, even in the daytime, this is one lonely stretch of road. I wasn't sure how far to go, so I picked a good spot to pull off the road where I could get a nice shot of Van Sciver Lake.

Ordinarily, Cindy would be the one to take the photos when we investigate a story, but this time she felt that I should take the pictures. I've learned from experience not to doubt her intuition when it comes to the paranormal and I'm happy to say it worked out once again.

While Cindy waited at the car, I walked over to the edge of the lake to see what would make a good shot. I ended up taking a half a dozen or so pictures of the lake and then a few pictures from up and down the road, just to give people an idea as to how isolated this area really was.

Just after taking some pictures on the road, I turned back towards the lake and snapped one last shot before getting in the car. I didn't know it at the time, but it was a good thing I took that last picture.

When I got home and was looking over the pictures on the computer, all of them came out normal. No Orbs. No Ectoplasm. No Apparitions – full body or otherwise. Except for one photo...the last one I had taken before leaving. This picture, and I'd love to put it in the book, but unfortunately you need to see it in color, not black and white. This picture has, what looks to me, a pink-colored mist in the center of it. Now what makes this so special is that according to lots of the eyewitnesses, Midnight Mary is wearing a pink prom dress or pink gown. I thought it was pretty amazing that the ectoplasm in the picture had a pink color to it. I've never gotten any kind of colored mist before in any pictures.

The next place on our agenda was to visit the graveyard where Gertrude Spring was buried to try to get a picture of her headstone. Using our GPS unit we made drive back to Bristol and tried to find the churchyard where she was buried. This proved to again, be trickier than I thought it would be. I had the name of the church, but not the exact address. St. James Church was on Cedar street.

The most difficult thing about driving in Bristol is that most of the streets only run one way in the downtown area. I had found Cedar Street, but we were too far down and had to loop back around in order to get to the section of the street where the church was located. Finally, after many twists and turns through small neighborhood streets, we reached our goal.

St. James Church is a small stone church surrounded by a small churchyard in the middle of a residential neighborhood. We were in luck that I was able to find a place to park on the street right near the gate to the churchyard. Since we had no clue as to where Gertrude Spring's grave site was, this was going to be a challenge.

We decided to split up so we could cover more ground. I took the area in front of the church and the right side of the churchyard, and Cindy searched the back of the churchyard and the left side between the church and the Parish House.

SIX

St. James Church has a few hauntings of its own.

Somewhere in this churchyard rests the mortal remains of Midnight Mary.

I had the easier of the area to search, because there weren't as many grave sites. I also lucked out and found a small box with bright neon green papers in it that had a printout of some of the graves so you could take a self-guided walking tour. Hopefully, this piece of information would help us locate Gertrude's grave.

We were the only people, (living) in the churchyard that day, so we didn't have to contend with others impeding our search. Cindy called out to me from the back of the churchyard and I quickly followed the sound of her voice to a grave that had a metal chair mounted in front of it. As cool as this discovery was, it wasn't what we were looking for. I had done some research and I found a reference to this chair called the "Witch's Chair."

The so-called "Witch's Chair" has an urban legend attached to it that goes something like this: If you sit in this chair at the stroke of midnight on Halloween night, the arms of a witch will reach out and surround and hold you to the chair. Another part of the legend says that if you sit in the chair, you'll have bad luck.

According to the walking tour pamphlet, there's a more mundane reason for the chair being there. This chair sits atop the grave of a man named Merritt Wright who died in 1911. Church legend has it that his widow Sarah Wright had the chair placed there so that she could rest her frail body when she came to visit his grave. The big question is where is Sarah Wright buried? She's not buried with her husband, Merritt, and since she was born in 1851, chances are she's not still alive. Thing is, nobody knows where she was buried.

As interesting as the iron chair was, I wanted to get back to the search for Gertrude's grave, so we went back to walking along the gravestones trying to get an idea of where she was buried. Finally, after several hours of searching, Cindy and I decided to give up. We'd scoured the churchyard from one end to the other and had no luck.

Looking to the church walking tour pamphlet was no help. They had some graves listed by number and marked with a small green flag, but sadly Gertrude's Grave wasn't one of them. According to the pamphlet, Gertrude Louise Spring died of a skull fracture in an automobile accident and she was laid to rest with other members of her family and given the full burial rite of the church.

When we returned home, I tried to do another Internet search for more information on Miss Spring, and of course, what do I find but a direct reference to where she's buried in the churchyard. So here's what I've found out. Maybe you'll have better luck finding her grave than we did that day. According to a source on the Internet, her grave is located between the church and the Parish House, near a slab of stone lying flat on the ground.

My quest for the grave of Midnight Mary may have turned up empty, but at least I have a possible photo of her spirit. Perhaps this trip wasn't a total loss after all.

> From Bristol, Pennsylvania: Go northeast on Pond Street, then turn left onto Jefferson Avenue. Get right onto US-13 North/Bristol Bypass, then turn right onto Fallsington Avenue. Turn left onto Main Street and stay straight until you reach Bordentown Road.

SIX

The Green Ghost Girl of Ireland

In May of 2010, Cindy and I took our first trip to the Republic of Ireland. It was our first trip to the Republic of Ireland and I have to admit it was fantastic. I have to say that we are not your typical type of tourist. As a rule, we generally don't do group tours and we usually strike out on our own and try to connect with the people and places you don't often see on a guided-group tour.

Keeping this in mind, we were in Ireland, a place neither of us had ever been to before and armed with some local maps, a rental car with a full tank of petrol (in other words: gas), and an open mind. We set out to explore southwestern Ireland on our terms for a week.

One of the first lessons we learned was: *Stay on the left side of the road!* Cindy was driving and I have to give her a round of applause. She picked up driving on the left much faster than I would have and also was very good at keeping pace with the local drivers that seemed to have a death wish. It's no wonder there are quite a few tales of ghostly hitchhikers in Ireland. The roads are so narrow I'd be scared to even walk alongside them in the daytime, let alone at night. As we drove from place to place we would see billboards from the Department of Transportation warning be people to slow down as "X" number of people had been killed on that road in the past couple of years. These numbers of highways fatalities were usually in the area of 40 to 70 deaths.

On our third day in Ireland, we actually broke one of our own travel rules and decided to go on a guided tour. I had heard of the Killarney Ghost Tours online before left home and I did want to do their tour while we were in Killarney. Oddly enough, as much trouble as we had finding our way around Killarney the first couple of days we there, we actually found the Ghost Tour people rather easily, as they were parked out on the main street with a very flashy-looking bus. They were very well organized and they had gone all-out to fix their bus up to look very creepy inside. Right as you walked in the door they had a life-size replica of some sort of crone or ghoul with glowing red eyes and a vaporous mist eerily swirled around your feet giving the whole inside of the vehicle an otherworldly atmosphere from the time you stepped on board. When

SECTION

we entered, there was a darkness lit only by ambient lighting, due to all the windows on the bus being curtained off. I had a strong feeling this was not going to be your typical ghost tour and I was right.

Once we were all seated, our guide the bus, he began to tell us of a ghost that would appear in people's cars anecdote that stood out in my mind coming back from playing a session

Sessions are what we would restaurant. Usually two or three Bohdran drum, or perhaps a tin

came back to our section of tale about a female apparition back in the late 1970s. One was about some musicians in Kenmare one night.

call a small gig in a bar or musicians playing a fiddle, whistle, will play at a pub

Some musicians had a late night encounter with the ghostly green girl right on this spot.
Courtesy of Cindy Wolf

SIX

for several hours to entertain the locals and tourists who happen to be there at the right time.

The three musicians were on the N7 heading back to Killarney from the town of Kenmare, which is to the south as they approached a sharp turn. Their car suddenly stopped in its tracks in the middle of the road right next to the old Derrycunnihy Church. They tried everything they could to get the car started. While they were fiddling with the engine, the air around them got icy cold. When they closed the hood they looked into the interior of the car and were surprised to see a girl wearing a green dress with long jet-black hair sitting in the back seat of the car. Her

SECTION

dress was not modern in any sense and she looked as though she was dripping wet from head to toe. She just stared at them and then, in the next instant, vanished into thin air. Never once opening the car door, she just vanished as quickly as she had appeared.

Still in shock and surprise, the three men quickly jumped back into the car and tried to start it once again. Much to their surprise and relief, it started right up as if there had never been anything wrong with it in the first place.

They drove to the nearest pub and proceeded to tell the pub owner what they had seen. After a few much-needed rounds of drinks, they finally calmed down enough for the Publican to explain what might have happened to them.

SIX

The Green Girl also has been known to make appearances at the Lake Hotel, in Killarney, Ireland. *Courtesy of Cindy Wolf*

It seems as though the three musicians were not the first ones to encounter the green-dressed girl's spirit on this stretch of road. Apparently, the girl's spirit is tied to the lake which runs alongside this road. Supposedly, the ghost is the daughter of one of the leaders of the MacCarthy-Mor clan who had died from drowning in a boating accident on the lake about 100 yards out from their castle, which is now in ruins and sits behind the Lake House Hotel. Not only is she supposed to haunt the road, but she has also been seen in room 206 in the Lake Hotel.

SECTION

The view of the MacCarthy-Mor Castle and the lake is very beautiful and scenic, especially at sunset, but aside from the wonderful view, we didn't catch anything paranormal. A few days later, Cindy and I visited both the Derrycunnhiy Church and the Lake Hotel just to see if we could get more of a feel for the area.

The Derrycunnhiy Church is just over a bridge with a very sharp turn. I personally would not have wanted to have my car break down on this stretch of road late at night. First of all, it's very isolated, and second, there would be no way for a car coming in either direction to be able to

The Green Girl is rumored to be connected with the McCarthy-Mor Clan who resided in this ruined castle.
Courtesy of Cindy Wolf

SIX

see you in time to stop. Even in the daytime, you have to pull off the road and into the small parking area next to the church to avoid being hit. There's no way someone could sneak up and get into someone's car without being seen. Even harder, would be to sneak away from someone's car without being seen in this area. They would have to have jumped over the bridge and into the water and that would have made a lot of noise in the daytime or at night. We pretty much concluded that whatever had happened to those musicians late one night out here on the road, it must have at least seemed paranormal to them, and without having been there, I can't really say that it wasn't.

Derrycunnhiy Church is on N71 in Killarney, Ireland. Follow N71 from downtown Killarney. It will take you past The Lake House Hotel and will take you directly to the Derrycunnhiy Church.

SECTION

Aircraft

SEVEN

In terms of transportation, compared to land-based vehicles, aircraft is still in its young adulthood stage. Even with all the modern technology, we are still trying to come up with even safer ways to fly.

Of course, there were some growing pains involved and there were a lot of mistakes made in designing aircraft to be better than the prior versions. Brave men and women had to test these new planes and some loss of life was inevitable.

There are many leftover planes in museums, airports, and air shows that have opted to adopt these outdated aircraft. There may be those that have gotten more than they bargained for. Some of these aircraft have a spirit or two attached to them that still feels the need to make its presence known.

Apparitions

SECTION 2

Flight 401

No chapter on haunted aircraft would be complete without an investigation into one of the most haunted accounts in aviation history – The Ghosts of Flight 401. When I was younger, I remember watching a television movie called *The Ghost of Flight 401*, featuring none other than William Shatner – AKA: Captain James T. Kirk of *Star Trek* fame. At the time, I thought it was just a movie, not realizing until years later that it was based on true events.

Flight 401 was an Eastern Airlines L-1011 Tristar Jumbo Jet that was a night flight scheduled to fly from New York to Miami. The jet crashed on December 29th, 1972 in the Florida everglades, a few miles from Miami International Airport. According to the official investigation into the accident, the crash was caused by a combination of equipment failure and pilot error. Evidently, there was a malfunction with the landing gear light and as both the Captain and 2nd officer were discussing the problem, they didn't notice that the plane was rapidly descending and would ultimately crash.

Not everyone died in the crash. Seventy people onboard, both passengers and crew would survive. But sadly, 101 people did die. Among the fatalities were the Pilot, Captain Robert Loft and 2nd Officer Don Repo. Both of these men would be at the heart of the ghostly legends that sprang from that tragic night.

Over the next several years, there would be many reports of ghostly sightings of both of these men. Most of them would occur on one particular plane: Eastern Airlines N318EA. The big question was: Why single this plane out of all the others in Eastern's fleet? At first, most people thought that it was because they were similar types of aircraft, both planes were L-1011s. They later found out a shocking secret, one that would explain at least part of the reason for the number of paranormal activities surrounding this plane. It was discovered that a number of parts salvaged from Flight 401 were installed on N318EA as it was being built. This was the final link to the *why* for the haunting of this plane.

Even though both Captain Loft and 2nd Officer Repo have been spotted on the 318 it's Don Repo that has been seen more often and has interacted with more people. In fact, it's the spirit of Don Repo who supposedly was in contact with author, John G. Fuller via Ouija board as he wrote the book: *The Ghost of Flight 401*.

SEVEN

The spirit of 2nd Officer Don Repo is supposed to be very concerned with the safety of the aircraft. Allegedly, he manifested to another pilot and told him point blank, "This plane will never crash. We won't let it happen." Perhaps he was talking about Captain Loft and all the other victims of the crash. In any case, it seems that the two officers were very emotionally attached to the parts of the 401 plane. Perhaps it's their guilt in being partially responsible for the crash and don't want to see it repeated.

On one flight, a woman passenger was seated next to an Eastern Airlines pilot who looked as though he was very ill. Concerned, she called for a stewardess to help him and then watched in surprise as the man dissipated before her eyes. I don't know about you, but I'd have been asking for another seat. Later, she identified the man as Don Repo from a photograph. I'm not sure what would upset me more: seeing someone vanish before my eyes or finding out I had been sitting next to a dead man. I'm also guessing that the person who showed her the picture had a hunch that it was Don Repo's spirit.

In another related incident on another flight, a female passenger was concerned about an unconscious man dressed as a Eastern Airlines Officer and called a stewardess for help. This time both the stewardess and the woman as well as several other passengers saw the man vanish. It seems that Don can't stop appearing to people.

A stewardess walked into the plane's galley one day and saw a man dressed as a flight engineer fixing one of the ovens. When she talked to the plane's flight engineer, he claimed that he hadn't had time to fix the oven. When she described what the other man looked like, the man realized that it must have been Don Repo.

I'm not sure what the fascination with the plane's ovens have to do with flight 401, but a lot of the ghostly encounters seem to happen in the galley area. Many times over the next few years, flight attendants would complain about how it was unnaturally cold in that area and how they always felt as though they weren't alone. Not only has Don Repo been spotted in that area of the plane, but other airline employees would claim to see people appear and vanish there.

A stewardess named Faye Merryweather saw the face of Don Repo staring at her from the glass out of the oven. She quickly found two other coworkers, one who had known Don Repo, and when they returned, the face was still there and her coworker identified the face as his. Then they heard a voice warn them that a fire would break out on board the plane later on in the flight. According to airline records, a fire did break out on this plane on the last leg of a flight returning from Mexico City and they had to cancel the remainder of the journey. It later was revealed that parts of the galley had been salvaged from Flight 401.

One final encounter with Don Repo took place when a flight engineer had boarded the plane to do a pre-flight check only to be greeted by a man dressed as a flight engineer who told him the work was already completed. The assigned flight engineer recognized Don Repo immediately, but before he could say anything, Repo vanished before his eyes.

Don Repo isn't the only active spirit of flight 401. The pilot, Captain Robert Loft has made a number appearances as well. Unlike Don Repo, Captain Loft seems to like making a quick guest appearance on board a plane, usually in the 1st-class cabin.

On one occasion, Captain Loft appeared to a pilot and two flight attendants shortly before plane 318 was due to take off from JFK airport from in New York.

Captain Loft once appeared to a stewardess who demanded to know who he was since, at the time, he wasn't authorized to be on board the plane. She left to get the Pilot and when she and the pilot confronted Captain Loft, the pilot recognized him immediately and then Loft vanished in full view of at least a dozen people. Things like this happened quite a bit on Plane #318 for those few years following the crash of Flight 401.

Not surprisingly, the management of Eastern Airlines frowned upon people talking about the ghost sightings and the official word was that anybody spreading tales of ghosts aboard any plane would be dismissed from employment. Despite the threat of dismissal, stories still managed to circulate throughout the airline industry.

I guessing it wasn't until they actually experienced it themselves that they might have been apt to be lenient with some of their employees experiences with the paranormal. An Eastern Airlines executive Vice-President was engaged in a conversation with a uniformed pilot in the first-class section of plane 318 one day when he suddenly realized that it was Captain Loft who vanished right in front of him – making the man a believer in all the ghostly tales that had been circulating about the plane.

Almost all of the eyewitnesses to Captain Loft's and Don Repo's manifestations agreed on one thing. That up until they pulled their vanishing act, they believed they were talking to a real flesh and blood person and not a spirit.

After several years of hearing about all these hauntings and trying to cover up plane log accounts of them, the upper management decided to prudently remove and replace the planes that had parts from Flight 401 with new parts. Strangely enough, once the new parts were in place, the hauntings stopped.

Shannon Airport's Fairy Ring

"The one thing you don't want to do is get the Wee Folk mad at you," said one particularly knowledgeable Killarney man as we waited to go on our ghost tour in the Southwestern Irish town of Killarney. "They'll do you a nasty turn, they will."

He continued to explain to us that certain areas of Ireland the Fairy Folk claim as their own, and if you are rash and stupid enough to disturb those places, then be prepared for all sorts of bad luck and misfortune to follow you until you appease them or they forget about you. But, beware. The Fair Folk have long memories and even longer lives.

There are several different types of areas the Wee Folk have claimed over the centuries. Some are very well known and others are hidden and are usually found merely by accident. If you see a white Hawthorn tree isolated in the middle of a farmers field, that's usually a good indication that it's a spot claimed by the Fair Folk.

Another type of Fairy plot of land is known as a Fairy Fort. These look like innocent round mounds of dirt usually in the shape of two concentric circles. Most of the time, it's easy to avoid them as they are usually in obscure places, but every once in a while, one will be discovered where civilization has encroached into the wilderness.

At Shannon International Airport, they recently discovered one of these Fairy Forts and unlike some land developers who would have just plowed it over and kept right on building, the officials at the airport took a different approach. Instead of building a new runway over the Fairy Fort they took a more open-minded point a view and decided to build their new runway in a manner that wouldn't disturb the Fairy Fort and thus not anger the Wee Folk. So far it seems to be working.

> Shannon International Airport is in County Clare, Ireland. The airport is 24 KM from Limerick, Ireland and 22KM from Ennis, Ireland.

SECTION

SEVEN

Shannon Airport officials took no chances when confronted with a fairy fort and built their new runway without disturbing it. *Courtesy of Cindy Wolf*

SECTION

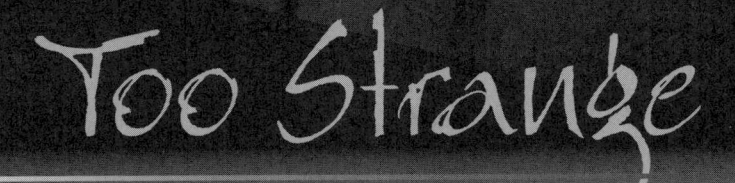

Too Strange

This corner of the mysterious Bermuda Triangle is on the Island of Bermuda.
Courtesy of Cindy Wolf

EIGHT

Sometimes I come across some bit of research for a book that just doesn't seem to fit into any one category. Yet, I don't want to leave these stories out because most of the time they do have some kind of relevance to what I was trying to get at with the overall topic. This next section is one of those areas that generally fall into the too weird to classify section. For example: The Bermuda Triangle has swallowed up both ships and planes so how could I put it in one or the other sections? I wanted to add these tales of the paranormal to this book because each story, in its own way, does relate to traveling in some way.

to Classify

SECTION 2

The Bermuda Triangle

No book on haunted travel would be complete without a look at the phenomenon know as The Bermuda Triangle. Strange things have been happening to planes and boats in this mysterious triangle of ocean since the days of Christopher Columbus.

But, what is the Bermuda Triangle? It's an area of the Atlantic Ocean that stretches from the island of Bermuda to Puerto Rico and then goes to Fort Lauderdale, Florida.

The first modern encounter with this strange area occurred during WWII. On December 5, 1945, five Avenger torpedo bombers took off from Fort Lauderdale, Florida, and were never seen again. A flying boat sent to look for the missing bombers also disappeared into the Bermuda Triangle. With more planes, a five-day search and rescue mission searched 250,000 miles of ocean and failed to turn up any sign of the missing vehicles.

Over the years, dozens of boats and planes have vanished without a trace, and to top it off, strange lights going back as far a Columbus's voyage have been spotted in the triangle. But what is going on here? Is it some kind of rip in the fabric of reality? Are aliens abducting ships and planes? Or is there a completely rational, but unknown reason for all these disappearances? That's what I intend to examine in this chapter.

Some Explanations

There are several theories about what happens in the Bermuda Triangle, also known as the Devil's Triangle. Here are some of the supernatural explanations. Granted, they may seem farfetched and fantastic, but stranger things have happened in other places.

The Sinking of Atlantis

One of the most popular supernatural theories is that leftover advanced super-science from Atlantis is the cause of all the disappearances, with the discovery of an underwater structure called the Bimini Road. Some archaeologists claim that the Bimini Road, which is located in the Bahamas near the Island of Bimini, is nothing more than a natural rock formation. Other, feel that it may be part of what's left over from the sinking of Atlantis. Regardless of what it is, it is supposedly inside the confines of the Bermuda Triangle and therefore what it has to do with the missing ships and planes should be taken into account. I mean really, with all the disappearances you would think that people would literally want to leave no stone unturned to discover what is going on.

Green Water, Compasses, The Gulf Stream, and On and On...

Some of the planes and ships that have vanished claim that right before they disappeared, there was something wrong with the water. They talk about white water turning green (whatever that is supposed to mean). Some pilots have radioed about having compass problems. Could it be extraterrestrial aliens causing some sort of disturbance? Possibly. Just remember, Christopher Columbus's crew also mention seeing strange lights in the sky inside the Bermuda Triangle and that was back in 1492.

Scientist and skeptics that can't bring themselves to even think that there might even be a non-scientific reason for the Bermuda Triangle have come up with several of their own theories as to what the causes are for many of these missing planes and boats.

The normal explanation for why compasses go haywire in the Bermuda Triangle is that these are normal magnetic fluctuations and have nothing to do with the supernatural or extraterrestrial origin. Scientist claim that there is a natural fluctuation in the magnetic poles both north and south, and because of this, compasses will not always point to true north, except in certain areas of the world.

One of my favorite debunking theories is the Gulf Stream. People think that because of the current of the Gulf Stream, boats and planes that have sunk or crashed might have been moved out of the Bermuda Triangle because of this current. This current is supposed to run from the Gulf of Mexico to the Northern Atlantic ocean. My question is: If that's so, then wouldn't it be a simple task to search along the course of the Gulf Stream, looking for wreckage or remains of these vehicles? Wouldn't there be a large quantity of these vessels dumped into the North Atlantic? If they can find the *Titanic* all the way on the ocean floor, you'd think we might be able to find some trace of these missing vessels. Right?

Human Error or Deliberate Destruction?

Human error and deliberate destruction have also been proposed as causes for disappearances in the Bermuda Triangle. Okay, granted people make mistakes, but can as many people that have been lost really be that careless? One documented case of human error, such as the loss of the S.S. *VA Foggy* in 1972 can be accounted for but, I don't see it happening all the time.

Now deliberate destruction I can see happening. We humans are a pretty violent bunch and one of our favorite pastimes, if you look back in history, is killing each other. So could deliberate attacks be the cause of some of the disappearances? Sure. Even I can admit that. But do I think that every disappearance is due to a ship or plane being attacked? In a word: No.

Piracy?

Piracy on the high seas was very rampant from the 1700s to the early twentieth century but, I think that even though you still hear of cases or today, I don't think modern-day pirates are the cause of so many missing vessels.

Weather

Another theory is that the ships and planes that have gone missing in the Bermuda Triangle are due to hurricanes. Again, I can see that maybe some ships and planes have been lost due to a massive hurricane. But, I still can't see how people can contribute every missing plane and ship to a hurricane. From what I understand, a lot of these vessels didn't disappear during any kind of severe weather occurrence.

Methane Hydrate

One of the best "rational explanations" with far-fetched stretches of credibility I've heard would have to be the Methane Hydrate theory. A Methane Hydrate is an eruption of natural gas that seeps up from a crack in the ocean floor that causes the water to bubble in a way that creates a buoyancy vacuum where a ship could lose its floatabilty and rapidly sink. This theory would work out great except for one problem: Even though there is one of these Methane Hydrates on the eastern coast of the United States, and it's in the vicinity of the Bermuda Triangle, it hasn't had an eruption for the last 15,000 years! So much for that bright idea.

The Incidents

Cindy and I usually take at least one cruise to Bermuda every couple of years, and yes, we have traveled through the Bermuda Triangle several times. So far, we haven't encountered anything stranger than me having a bout of seasickness on our last trip (thank God for Dramamine and sea bands). But, I keep hoping that maybe we'll see something paranormal one of these days. That having been said, I'd like to examine some of the more interesting incidents that have happened to people in the Bermuda Triangle.

Flight 19

The most famous incident, and the one that has sparked the most controversy is the disappearance of the doomed Flight 19 out of Fort Lauderdale, Florida, on December 5, 1945. The squadron of Avenger Torpedo Bombers left that day on a routine training mission.

The training mission was led by veteran pilot, Lt. Charles Carroll Taylor. They were supposed to head out over the Atlantic and then return. Problem is, that never happened. During the mission, the squadron experienced compass anomalies and Lt. Taylor radioed that something looked wrong with the water. Shortly after that last transmission the planes disappeared.

The base launched a search and rescue plane in order to find the missing Flight 19 and the thirteen-man crew, not to mention the Mariner Aircraft they were flying also went missing and was never recovered. The navy has classified these disappearances as: Unsolved.

DC-3

A few years later, on December 28, 1948, a DC-3 airplane, flying from San Juan, Puerto Rico, to Miami, Florida, vanished in the Bermuda Triangle with thirty-two people on board. No explanation was ever given for this disappearance either.

USS Cyclops

The armed forces suffered the loss of the USS *Cyclops* in 1918. With the loss of 309 crew members, it is still considered the largest single loss of life outside of combat in U.S. Naval history. Aside from the fact that it was in the Bermuda Triangle, no other explanation has been forthcoming.

The USS *Cyclops* vanished after leaving Barbados on March 4, 1918.

Theodosia Burr

Even stranger is the case of Theodosia Burr, daughter of Vice President Aaron Burr. She was a passenger aboard the *Patriot*. Her voyage was supposed to leave Charleston, South Carolina, and arrive in New York on December 30, 1812, but it never arrived. No one knows what ever happened to the ship or the crew.

After doing research for this book, I have noticed a pattern to these disappearances and maybe I'm not the first person to do so; but from what I can see, a majority of these missing planes and ships have vanished in the Bermuda Triangle during the wintertime. Perhaps whatever is causing these disappearances has a limited span of time when it's active. In any case, no matter what the cause, the Bermuda Triangle continues to be a mystery to this day.

The Bermuda triangle stretches from Bermuda to Fort Lauderdale, Florida, and then to San Juan, Puerto Rico.

The Greenbriar Light

In Jacksonville, Florida, there's a phenomenon know as the Greenbriar Light. As ghost lights go, this one seems to be fairly active and as yet still remains a mystery. This strange ball of light seems to be attracted to moving objects, such as slow-moving cars and people walking.

This is where the Greenbriar Light is known to follow cars.

This ball of light is supposed to be the manifestation of a phantom motorcyclist. The light itself is thought to be the headlight of the motorcycle. As the story goes, a man was testing the limits of a brand new motorcycle on this road when he lost control and skidded into the support wire of a telephone pole at a breakneck speed and beheaded himself. His decapitated body wasn't found until the next day. Now his spirit is trying to reconnect his missing body parts and the light helps him.

According to a number of posts by people on the Internet, the Greenbriar Light will appear almost all the time. If you turn your car headlights off and drive slowly down Ghost Light Road, as it's called, the light will trail you by between 25 to 300 feet. Sometimes, according to a blogger, it will pass you; then the light changes from white to red as you're now looking at the taillights of the motorcycle.

A ghostly motorcyclist has been known to ride behind cars on this stretch of highway in northern Florida.

Due to all the reports about this light, in 1987, The St. John County Sheriff's Department called in some scientists to try and determine what rational cause for the Greenbriar Light might be. Try as they might, the scientific team could come up with no solid explanation for the phenomenon.

When Cindy and I drove to this road, we were surprised to find it a fairly busy highway. In fact, when you drive onto Greenbriar Road you may not have even realized that you changed roads from your previous road. At one point, the main road splits to the left and continues. Greenbriar Road is the one straight ahead. We had been on Greenbriar Road for several yards before I realized where we were. I had Cindy stop the car so I could take some pictures. Not that Greenbriar Road is anything spectacular, it looks like a normal two lane highway with woods on either side. I had read that Greenbriar Road was some sort of dirt back road, but this was a modern two-lane road, although there was a dirt road leading off from it to my right.

As I learned on Bordentown Road hunting for Midnight Mary, it's best to take a picture even if you don't have any idea of what you might get on film. So I snapped off a few pictures as I looked around the roads. Unfortunately, there was no sign of a ghost light on any of them that we could see with our own eyes. To be honest, if this is the road, then I'm not sure how people could tell a ghost light from a regular headlight. But for the sake of thoroughness, I looked over the area for any clues to where this mysterious light could be originating from; but to tell the truth, I couldn't see any man-made source that could produce the sort of effect people have described in the past.

From Jacksonville: Greenbriar road is in St. John's County. It's a normal stretch of road between Switzerland and Orangeville, Florida.

SECTION

This dirt road could lead to the source of the Greenbriar Light.

The St. Augustine Lighthouse

Why add a haunted lighthouse to a book on haunted travel you might ask? Simple. Lighthouses are a very necessary part of naval travel. They are beacons of safety and warning to traveling vessels, and the St. Augustine Lighthouse is not only one of the oldest lighthouses in the country, it is also one of the most haunted.

One of the oldest and most haunted lighthouses in the United States. *Courtesy of Cindy Wolf*

EIGHT

The current lighthouse is not the first lighthouse that existed in this spot. But it is the one that is haunted to this day. This particular lighthouse was built in 1874 and has several different hauntings from different time periods. Not only is the lighthouse haunted, but the lighthouse keeper's house has a history of being haunted also. The grounds around the lighthouse and the keeper's house have also been known to have weird lights and auditory paranormal activity, that has been so active that T.A.P.S. has been there and declared it definitely haunted.

So what makes this particular lighthouse so haunted? A good question, and in order to answer it, we'll have to take a look into the long and diverse history of the lighthouse.

Because of it's prime location on Anastasia Island, there has always been some sort of beacon here since the 1500s. Originally, there was just a forty-foot-high wooden watchtower decked out with signal flags and a primitive light. This served its purpose of guiding ships for over 300 years before it was decided that a more permanent structure was necessary.

The St. Augustine Lighthouse had the reputation of being haunted from the very beginning of its construction. There's a long-standing maritime tradition that says lighthouses naturally attract the souls of the dead that have died at sea, acting as beacon for them to find their way back to solid land. If all the reports about the St. Augustine Lighthouse are true, it's definitely living up to reputation. Perhaps this is why most paranormal researchers consider the lighthouse as one of the top ten active sites in Florida.

It wasn't until 1824 that a real lighthouse existed on the spot; built out of wood and stone, this lighthouse was the first one ever erected in Florida.

The lighthouse that exists now was constructed between the years 1871 and 1874. It's in this period of time that the most active hauntings have their origin.

According to local folklore, two of the most active spirits that haunt the lighthouse and the surrounding grounds are little girls. It seems that during the construction of the current lighthouse, a small track and railroad handcar would be used to transport building materials from the shore to the construction site. It is said that the two young daughters of the lighthouse keeper, liked to play roller coaster with the handcart. What they would do, almost on a daily basis, is climb inside the handcar and release the brake, riding the cart down to the end of the track where

SECTION

These woods just outside the light keeper's house are full of orbs and paranormal energy. *Courtesy of Cindy Wolf*

there was an automatic brake that stopped it from plunging into the ocean. Except, one day, whoever was in charge of securing the brake at the shore end forgot to set it the night before. I'm sure you can see where this is going.

The next morning as usual, the girls, giggling and laughing, climbed into the handcar and released the break, not realizing that it would be the last ride of their lives. Tragically, the car failed to stop, and to the surprise and horror of the workers, they witnessed the handcart run off the tracks and plunge into the ocean. The cart overturned trapping the scared little girls underwater. The workers raced to the scene of the accident, but sadly, the two girls had drowned under the weight of the handcar before anyone could reach them.

EIGHT

There is another version of how the girls drowned. The story goes that the girls were playing in the surf when either a large wave or a strong undertow dragged them out to sea and they drowned. Either way it happened, the end result was that two little girls had lost their lives, and from that time forward, their young spirits have been seen and heard in and around the St. Augustine Lighthouse.

These two little girl's spirits were soon joined by a third girl's spirit. In the early 1900s, a ten- or eleven-year-old girl was struck and killed by a steam train. Her spirit tends to make its presence known on the grounds of the lighthouse. Many times she'll be spotted near the bushes next to the tower. Her disembodied footsteps have also been heard crunching the gravel paths that surround the lighthouse grounds.

On a recent trip to Florida, Cindy and I decided to spend a few days in St. Augustine. Cindy has been there quite a few times, since she had lived in Florida before we met and felt that I would really like St. Augustine because of its historic and ghostly history.

To say that St. Augustine embraces its haunted history would be a great understatement. Outside of Gettysburg, Pennsylvania, I don't know of any other city that has the number of walking ghost tours, ghost train tours, or ghostly trolley tours that St. Augustine has. Even the St. Augustine Lighthouse gives ghost tours on certain nights during the week.

Cindy and I took several ghost tours while we were there, but only one of them went as far as the St. Augustine Lighthouse. The "Doomed Trolley" took us and about fifty other people out to the grounds surrounding the St. Augustine Lighthouse, and our ghostly tour guide, Jordan, told us some of the stories she'd heard about the lighthouse, including the one I've already mentioned about the little girl spirits. She mentioned that there is a male spirit that is also associated with the area around the lighthouse and the keeper's house.

During the early 1930s, a man believed to have been severely depressed over his financial losses during the stock market crash of 1929, wandered out to the old lighthouse keeper's house and proceeded to commit suicide by hanging himself from one of the rafters in the old building. It's been said that on particularly stormy nights, you can see his spirit lurking about the premises, or when the house is exceedingly dark, the ghastly sight of his body hanging from one of the wooden rafters has been spotted on occasion.

SECTION

We were left off the trolley on the grounds of the St. Augustine Lighthouse. As we wandered among a few of the trees outside of the keeper's house, it was very easy to see why it had such a haunted reputation. We had toured the lighthouse and keeper's house earlier that day and at night it took on a whole new darker aspect.

Cindy managed to catch quite a few orbs among the trees. We also noticed that there were some strange energy ribbons in the distance in a few of her pictures; something we hadn't come across before. I can say that even though I wasn't taking any pictures, I could feel that there was something not quite normal in the area. For one thing, it was much colder than anywhere else we had been that night. Now, it could just have been the breeze coming off the water, but I had a feeling there was more to it than that easy explanation. As I wandered through the trees, I took a good look at the light keeper's house while Cindy wandered around snapping various photos in hopes of getting an apparition or maybe some ectoplasm.

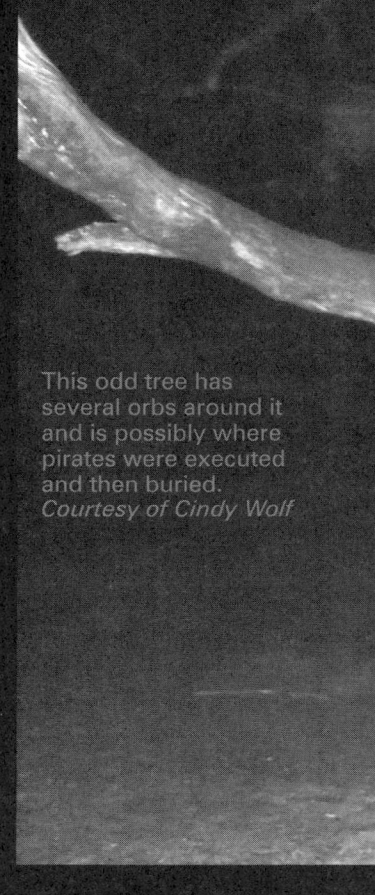

This odd tree has several orbs around it and is possibly where pirates were executed and then buried.
Courtesy of Cindy Wolf

I thought back to some of the other stories I'd heard about this lighthouse. There was the story about a former lighthouse keeper who had died on the spiral staircase leading up to the top of the lighthouse. They say he was carrying a bucket of kerosene. Carrying those buckets could very well bring on a heart attack. It's a long walk (219 steps) to the top of the lighthouse and not an easy task if you're out of shape. They say the man's spirit still makes that walk up the stairs on certain nights and many people have heard the sounds of a kerosene bucket dropping on the stairs and the sounds of heavy footsteps echoing throughout the interior of the lighthouse.

If you happen to be in the St. Augustine area, make sure you take some time to take a trip out to the old lighthouse. With so many different spirits, it's more than likely that you'll pick up something on your camera.

EIGHT

The St. Augustine Lighthouse on Anastasia Island. It's right off Highway A1A. The address is 81 Lighthouse Avenue.

Appendix A

A Word About Orbs and Other Photographic Anomalies

I know I've touched on this subject in other places is this book and in my other two volumes, but I wanted to devote a whole chapter to this subject because there's a large debate in the Paranormal Community concerning the validity of orbs and images in digital pictures.

I know most people have heard of this phenomenon, but just what is spirit photography and how did it start?

Spirit photography is the attempt to capture a picture of a ghost or spirit on film. Most paranormal investigators use a still-photo camera as well as camcorders to try and capture the image of a ghost that may not be visible to the naked eye. This technique has been around since the early days of photography back in the 1800s.

The first person to try to photograph a spirit was a man named Mr. Mummler who was taking a photograph of himself and discovered, quite back accident, that there was another figure in the picture with him. It was just a double image, which happened fairly often back in the early days of photography, because you had to sit for long periods of time in order to get a picture to expose on the negative. Early developing techniques also had a lot of room for error. Despite the fact that this was an obvious fraudulent picture, he developed a system that made it seem as though there were spirits appearing in photographs. People ate this stuff up. There was a big spiritualist movement back then and séances were popular. Even Mary Todd Lincoln was a firm believer in contacting spirits. There's a famous Mummler photo of her with the supposed spirit of Abe Lincoln standing behind her.

However, just because Mummler faked his photographs doesn't mean that all spirit photographs are fakes. People have been doctoring up photos and film since the process was invented. Usually, if there's a will, there's a way to fake a photograph. As a Fuji certified photo specialist, it was my job to figure out what made pictures develop badly, whether it was a light leak from a faulty camera, a bad flash unit, poor lighting, double exposed film or any other of a hundred problems. Sometimes, you would just get a picture that you couldn't explain. Not that we didn't try. (Just to become certified I had to take a test and if I even got one question wrong I had to take the entire exam over again.)

I literally have looked at thousands and thousands of photos and have seen almost every kind of photographic aberration in existence. Don't get me wrong, I'm not saying that every orb photo is a paranormal phenomenon. Yes, it is very easy to fake those orbs, and if you don't know the conditions in which the photo was taken, then you have to take it with a grain of salty skepticism.

Photoshop and other photo-enhancing computer programs can make some convincing digital fake ghost photos at first glance. Those photos should come under strict judgment. The photos that I generally think are harder to fake, but not impossible, are the ones taken with regular film that has to be developed from negatives, though there are darkroom tricks you can pull to fake those types of pictures, too. However, they are much easier to detect and harder for a regular person to pull off without extensive developing skill.

So, in conclusion, don't believe everything you see presented to you as a ghost photograph, but also don't automatically dismiss all ghost photos. Especially the ones you've taken yourself and know what the conditions were when you were snapping the picture.

Appendix B

Ghost Tours

I am in no way connected with the following ghost tour companies. Cindy and I have gone on these tours as customers and found them very interesting. I hope you find them interesting as well. Bear in mind that most ghost tours in general are for merely entertainment purposes. You will not be going on a serious paranormal investigation. Most ghost tours usually last an hour or so and will sometimes include a lot of walking in the dark. So if you are physically challenged, call the tour group first and find out what special arrangements can be made for you.

Another point that I should mention is that most tour groups are made up of at least a dozen people or more, so if you're expecting a small group, you'd be better off booking a private ghost tour for your individual party.

Ghost tours are fun, informative, and sometimes a little spooky, and you may capture a spirit on film...or not. Be wary of ghost tours that "guarantee" you'll see a ghost. Most spirits do not appear on demand.

Here is a list I've compiled of ghost tours that are in some of the places I've written about in this book. This is by no means a complete list, just a sampling of what's out there.

When possible I've included contact information, including a phone number and website where than can be reached. As of this printing all contact information is up to date.

Ghost Tours of Strasburg
Strasburg, Pennsylvania
Phone: 717-687-6687
Website: www.ghosttour.com

Strasburg Rail Road Walking Ghost Tour
Strasburg, Pennsylvania
Phone: 717-687-7522
Website: www.strasburgrailroad.com/walking-ghost-tour.php

Market Ghost Tour
Seattle, Washington
Phone: 206-805-0195
Website: www.seattleghost.com

Underground Tour
Seattle, Washington
Phone: 206-682-4646
Website: www.undergroundtour.com

Haunted Vegas Tours
Las Vegas, Nevada
Phone: 702-339-8744
Website: www.hauntedvegastours.com

Ghosts and Goodtime Girls Walking Tour
Skagway, Alaska
Website: www.redonion1898.com/tour

The Original Killarney Ghost Tour
Killarney, Ireland
Phone: 087-2945007
Website: www.killarneyghosttour.com

Ghost Tours of Harpers Ferry
Harpers Ferry, West Virginia
Phone: 304-725-8019
Website: www.harpersferryghost.20.m.com

Ghosts and Gravestones Frightseeing Tour
St. Augustine, Florida
Phone: 904-826-3663
Website: www.ghostsandgravestones.com/st.augustine

Ripley's Ghost Train Adventure
St. Augustine, Florida
Phone: 904-824-1606
Website: www.ghosttrainadventure.com

Dark of the Moon Tour
St. Augustine, Florida
Phone: 904-829-0745 Ext. 207
Website: www.staugustinelighthouse.com

Ghost Walk of Cobh
Cobh, Ireland
Phone: +353 21 4815211
Website: www.titanic-trail.com

Paranormal Spirit Walk-Queen Mary
Long Beach, California
Phone: 877-342-0738
Website: www.queenmary.com

Ghosts of Gettysburg
Gettysburg, Pennsylvania
Phone: 717-337-0445
Website: www.ghostsofgettysburg.com

Sources

Bibliography

Books

Adams III, Charles J. and Seibold, David J., *Ghost Stories of the Lehigh Valley*, Exeter House Books, Reading, PA, 1993

Adams III, Charles J., *Ghost Stories of Chester County and The Brandywine Valley*, Exeter House Books, Reading, PA, 2001

Adams III, Charles J., *Ghost Stories of Berks County*, Exeter House Books, Reading, PA, 1982

Adams III, Charles J., *Bucks County Ghost Stories*, Exeter House Books, Reading, PA, 1999

Belanger, Jeff, *Encyclopedia of Haunted Places*, New Page Books, Franklin Lakes, NJ, 2005

Belanger, Jeff, *The World's Most Haunted Places*, New Page Books, Franklin Lakes, NJ, 2004

Berlitz, Charles, *Charles Berlitz's World of Strange Phenomena*, Ballentine Books, NY, 1988

Brown, Stephen D., *Spooky Harpers Ferry*, The Little Brown House, Harpers Ferry, WV, 1976

Caplan, Bruce M., *The Sinking of the Titanic*, Seattle Miracle Press Inc., Bellevue, WA, 1997

Cohen, Daniel, *The Encyclopedia of Ghosts*, Avon Books, New York, NY, 1984

Gilbert, David T., *A Walker's Guide To Harpers Ferry West Virginia*, Harpers Ferry Historical Association, Harpers Ferry, WV, 1995

Guiley, Rosemary Ellen, *The Encyclopedia of Ghosts and Spirits*, Facts On File, Inc., New York, NY, 1992

Hauck, Dennis William, *Haunted Places, The National Directory*, Penguin Books, New York, NY, 1996

Jenkins, Greg, *Florida's Ghostly Legends and Haunted Folklore*, Vol. 2, Pineapple Press, Inc., Sarasota, FL, 2005

Lake, Matt, *Weird Pennsylvania*, Sterling Publishing Co. Inc., New York, NY, 2005

Matusiak, Elizabeth, *The Battlefield Dead, State of the Art*, Denver, CO, 2000

Norman, Michael, and Scott, Beth, *Historic Haunted America*, Tom Doherty Associates, Inc., New York, NY, 1995

Oberding, Janice, *The Haunting of Las Vegas*, Pelican Publishing Co., Gretna, LA, 2008

Periodicals

Rickenbach, Joel, "Eerie PA, Issue 1," Eerie PA, West Chester, PA, 2005
St. Augustine Tour Guide
St. James Cemetery-Walking Tour

Websites

www.wikipedia.org
http://en.wikipedia.org/wiki/phantom_vehicle
www.theshadowlands.net
www.ghosteyes.com

Places Index

Adamstown, Pennsylvania, 12, 14, 16, 17
Addamsburry, 12
Agua Caliente, 77
Alaska, 18, 22, 23, 59, 60
Anastasia Island, 147
Anza Barrego State Park, 77, 78
Arkansas, 109
Atlantic City, New Jersey, 88
Atlantic Ocean, 86, 136
Atlantis, 137
Athens, Greece, 88
Bahamas, 137
Barbados, 140
Battalion, Alabama, 33
Battle of Gettysburg, 99, 101
Battle of Mount Hope, 34
Battle of Winchester, 76
Battle of Seattle, 19, 20
Baumstown, Pennsylvania, 103
Beggertown, 64
Berks County, Pennsylvania, 103, 104, 105
Bermuda Triangle, The, 135-139
Bermuda Underwater Institute, 89
Big Bend Mountain, 54, 55
Big Bend Tunnel, 56
Bimini Road, 137
Birdsboro, Pennsylvania, 103, 104, 105
Blue Diamond Road, 39
Blockbuster Video, 63
Bollman Hat Factory, 12, 15, 16
Borough of Adamstown, 12
Borough of Strasburg, 64
Boot Road, 29, 32
Bordentown Road, 112-115, 143
Boston, Massachusetts, 69
Brandywine Creek, 31, 32
Branson, Missouri, 88
Bridgeport, Pennsylvania, 63
Bristol, Pennsylvania, 115, 116
Brooklyn Bridge, 97
Bujno Pottery, 14
Butterfield Road, 77

Carcross, Yukon, 60
Carrizo Wash Station, 77, 79
Cedar Grove Cemetery, 13
Cemetery Ridge, 98
Charlestown, South Carolina, 140
Chicago, Illinois, 8, 11
Chesapeake & Ohio Railroad, 54, 55
Chester County, Pennsylvania, 31, 32
Cholame, California, 71
Clanton, Alabama, 108
Clairmont's Cabinet Making Shop, 21
Club 662, 36
Coatesville Service Building, 32
Cobh, Ireland, 156
County Road 25, 34
Cullman, Alabama, 109
Cry Baby Hollow, 109
Daytona, Florida, 70
Derrycunnihy Church, 121, 124, 125
Devil's Den, 98
Dip, The, 34, 35
Doc Maynard's Public House, 23-25
Downingtown, Pennsylvania, 29, 32
Downtown Seattle, 19
East Earl, Pennsylvania, 115
East Petersburg, Pennsylvania, 66
Eiffel Tower, 61
El Paso, Texas, 77
England, 6
Entenach Distillery, 15
FADO, 27
Fairfield Road, 98
Federal Arsenal, 47
Fitchburg, Massachusetts, 55
Flamingo Casino Hotel, 37, 38
Flamingo Road, 37
Flying Dutchman, 77, 83
Fort Lauderdale, Florida, 136, 139
French Creek, 41, 43, 44
Front Street, 21
Garden City, Long Island, 9
Gettysburg, Pennsylvania, 6, 64, 97-99, 149

Georgia Aquarium, 86-88
Ghost Light Road, 142
Golden North Hotel, 60
Great Seattle Fire, The, 20
Greenbriar Road, 142, 143
Hamilton, Bermuda, 89
Harper's Ferry, West Virginia, 45-51
Harper's Ferry National Historic Site, 51
Haunted Las Vegas Ghost Tours, 38
Hell's Hole, 64
Highway 4, 70
Highway 12, 56
Highway 666, 11
Highway of Death, 39
Hinton, West Virginia, 54
Henry Hill, 34
Hershey, Pennsylvania, 33
Hog Alley, 49-51
Hoosic Tunnel, 55
Hopewell Forge State Historical Site, 105
Jacksonville, Florida, 141
James Dean Memorial, 74
James River & Kanawha Canal Co., 54
Jefferson County, West Virginia, 51
J.F.K. International Airport, 130
John Brown's Fort, 47, 48
Kingsport Hospital, 81
Kingsport, Tennessee, 81
Kenmare, Ireland, 120, 121
Kennedy Farmhouse, 46
Killarney, Ireland, 119, 121, 123, 125, 131
Knauertown, Pennsylvania, 44
Koval Street, 37
Lake House Hotel, 123-125
Lancaster County, Pennsylvania, 12, 64, 66
Las Vegas, Nevada, 36, 38-40, 89
Little Round Top, 98
London, England, 91
Long Beach, California, 92, 95
Los Angeles, California, 73
Louisa County, Virginia, 54
Louisa Railroad, 54
Luxor, 85, 86, 89-91
MacCarthy Mor Castle, 124
Madison Avenue, 21
Main Street, 12-17, 64, 105
Marsh Creek, 98-100
Maryland, 51
Mason-Dixon Line, 46
MGM Grand Hotel and Casino, 36

Miami International Airport, 128
Miami, Florida, 73, 128
Missouri, 54
Mexico City, 129
Monterrey, Mexico, 88
Mount Hope, Alabama, 34
Mountain Springs Summit, 40
Mt. Jackson, 76
Muddy Run Creek, 66
Murderous Mile, The, 29, 30
Netherland Inn Road, 81
New England, 69
New York, 55, 128, 140
New York, New York, 88
New York Central Railroad, 57
Norwegian Cruise Lines, 59
Norwegian Pearl, 59
Old Birdsboro Bridge, 103-105
Orangeville, Florida, 143
Orlando, Florida, 70
Orlando/Daytona Highway, 70
Pahrump, Nevada, 39
Panama Canal, 61
Paradise, Pennsylvania, 63
Pasa Robles War Memorial Hospital, 72
Pennsylvania Dutch Country, 64, 98
Pennsylvania Ghost Hunters Society, 25, 99
Pennsylvania Railroad Museum, 64
Pentagon, 57
Philadelphia, Pennsylvania, 115
Pioneer Square, 23
Potomac River, 45, 51
Puerto Rico, 136
Quarry Road, 32
Red Onion Saloon, 60
Red Rock Canyon, 40
Republic of Ireland, 119
R.M.S. *Queen Mary*, 92-95
Route 23, 41
Route 160, 39
Sach's Mill Bridge, 97-99, 101
Sacramento, California, 78
Sacramento High School, 73
Salinas, California, 71
San Diego, California, 77
San Francisco, California, 71
San Juan, Puerto Rico, 139
Santa Barbara, California, 75
Santa Ynez, California, 75
Schuylkill River, 103, 106

Seattle, Washington, 18, 20, 22, 23, 25, 28
Seattle Underground Tour, 23, 24, 26, 28
Seattle Volunteer Fire Company, 21
Shannon International Airport, 131
Shenandoah River, 45, 51
Shenandoah Valley, 54
Sin City, 40
Skagua, 59, 60
Skagway, Alaska, 59-61
Solvang Road, 80
South Baumstown Road, 105
Southampton, England, 87
Springfield, Illinois, 57, 58
Starbucks, 26
State Route 41, 71
State Route 46, 71
Statue of Liberty, 61
Strasburg, Pennsylvania, 64, 67
Strasburg Railroad, 52, 63, 64, 67
St. James Episcopal Church, 114, 116, 117
St. Louis, Missouri, 78
St. Augustine, Florida, 149
St. Augustine Lighthouse, 146, 147, 149, 150
St. Peter's Road, 44
St. Peter's Village, 41, 42
St. Peter's Village Bakery, 43
St. Peter's Village Inn, 42-44
Switzerland, Florida, 143
Tampa, Florida, 70
Talcott, West Virginia, 55, 56
Trenton, New Jersey, 113
Tucson, Arizona, 91
Twin Tunnels, 29-32
United States, 88, 89, 109
U.S. Highway 11, 76
Van Sciver Lake, 112-115
Vallecito Station, 77-80
Virginia, 51
Virginia Central Railroad, 54, 55
Valley Creek Road, 29, 32
Washington, D.C., 57, 58
West Virginia, 51
Wilmington & Northern Railroad, 41
Winchester, Virginia, 76
World Trade Center, 57
Yukon & White Pass Railroad, 59-62
Yuma, 77, 78